# ESCAPE
## FROM IRAN

# ESCAPE
## FROM IRAN

ᏝᏉ

The Exodus of
Persian Jewry
During the Islamic
Revolution of 1979

## Sholem Ber Hecht

Published 2020 by Gildan Media LLC
aka G&D Media
www.GandDmedia.com

Front cover design by David Rheinhardt of Pyrographx

Interior design by Meghan Day Healey of Story Horse, LLC

Library of Congress Cataloging-in-Publication Data is available upon request

ISBN: 978-1-7225-0294-2

10  9  8  7  6  5  4  3  2  1

כֹּה אָמַר ה'... לְכָל־הַגּוֹלָה אֲשֶׁר־הִגְלֵיתִי מִירוּשָׁלַ‍ִם בָּבֶלָה:

כִּי־כֹה אָמַר ה' כִּי לְפִי מְלֹאת לְבָבֶל שִׁבְעִים שָׁנָה אֶפְקֹד אֶתְכֶם... לְהָשִׁיב אֶתְכֶם אֶל־הַמָּקוֹם הַזֶּה:

"Thus said Hashem, Master of Legions,
G-d of Israel, to all those exiled
from Jerusalem to Babylonia:

'Build houses, and settle;
plant gardens, and eat their fruits.'
'Take wives, and beget sons and daughters;
take wives for your sons . . .
'Flourish there . . .
'Seek the peace of the City to which I have exiled you,
and pray for it to Hashem . . .
'For through *its* peace, *you* shall have peace.
'. . . For when your seventy years in Babylonia
shall be complete, I will attend to you;
and I will fulfill for you My good word, My promise:
To return you to this place.'"

—*JEREMIAH 29:4-7, 10*

# CONTENTS

Ↄ∞თ

# PROLOGUE
## Exile To Exodus
⁂

In the book of Jeremiah, the Prophet Yermiyahu receives a prophetic vision from G-d that his mission shall be to serve as a "Prophet to the nations" of the world. The most powerful nation in the world at that time was the Kingdom of Babylon, under the rule of King Nebuchadnezzar, who had come to power during the waning years of the Jewish monarchy in Jerusalem. Yermiyahu was sent to the Yehudites, of the remaining Israelite Kingdom of Yehuda, with words of admonition and rebuke for their moral and societal decline. Yermiyahu gave stern warning to the Jews that if they failed to repent for their sinfulness in the service of G-d and drastically improve their unethical behavior, there would be terrible consequences: destruction, death, and exile.

After conquering the great metropolis of Nineveh, Nebuchadnezzar sent his General Nevuzaradan to lead his armies to the land of Israel. With much barbarism and bloodshed Nevuzaradan extended Babylonian hegemony over the Jewish state. At first, he allowed the Jewish monarchy to continue under his control, and appointed Yechonia as King of Yehuda. But Yechonia rebelled against Nebuchadnezzar; and thus began the process of *galut*—the exile of the Jewish people from the Land of Israel. As punishment for his intransigence, Yechonia was exiled to Babylon, together with members of the royal family and thousands of scholars, princes, ministers, and leaders of the Jewish people.

Subsequently, his uncle, Tzidkiyahu, was appointed as King in his place. But the process of exile continued over the next thirteen years, culminating in the destruction of the first Holy Temple in Jerusalem in the year 3338 after Creation.* This tragic chain of events reached its apex after the assassination of Gedalyah, the Yehudite puppet Governor appointed by Nebuchadnezzar, just one year after the Temple was destroyed. Eight hundred and fifty years after Moshe's disciple Yehoshua had trium-

---

* Seder Hadorot, dating the destruction in the year 3338, indicates that the number 338 is the *gematriya* (numerical equivalent) of the word *shalach*—"send out."

phantly led the tribes of Israel across the Jordan to conquer and inherit the Holy Land, the glory of the Jewish commonwealth and the majesty of the Jewish Kingdom came to a tragic close. Yermiyahu's prophetic vision did not end there. Together with his words of admonition he went on to instruct the exiles that once in Babylon, the refugees should find homes, marry, raise families, and settle in the lands of exile. Babylonia, Persia, and Medea—known collectively as *galut Bavel*, or *galut Bavel/Paras*—became the home-in-exile for the displaced People of the Book. Yermiyahu further prophesied that the *galut* would end after seven decades of exile, when there would be a Redemption, and a return to Zion.

So *galut Bavel/Paras*, or so it seemed, was supposed to be short-lived: the Jews would soon return to the Holy Land and rebuild the Temple. But even Yermiyahu's prophecies could not fathom the mysterious ways by which the promised Redemption would actually play out. It took the Prophetess Queen Esther, and her guardian, Mordechai Hayehudi, the spiritual giant of his generation, to write, direct, and perform the ensuing acts of the drama.

My dear departed friend Mr. Khalil Moradi of Forest Hills, New York, a man who (as we shall see) played a pivotal and heroic role in the modern-day adventure we called *"Escape from Iran,"* proudly traced his origins to a city in Iran named Hamedan. In ancient times Hamedan was named Shushan, the capital city of the Persian Kingdom. He remembered visiting the tombs of Mordechai and Esther there, of which he spoke with reverence and fervor. Each Purim, he reveled in the biblical Book of Esther's dramatic story of our miraculous salvation from attempted genocide, as though it were his own family annals.

There was indeed a return to the Holy Land, and the Temple was in fact rebuilt, as predicted. But its light was less bright than the light of the First Temple; and there were more tribulations to come; and in so many ways our inner sense of being a displaced, still-servile nation has remained with us. Those seventy years in Babylon/Paras became a prelude to twenty-five centuries of ongoing exile.

The long saga of Persian Jewry that began more than 2,500 years ago continues to unfold in the turmoil that is modern day Iran. Though Babylonia served as a glorious center of Jewish life and Torah scholarship for centuries, *Bavel/Paras* is not what it once was. Nevertheless, the presence of a vibrant Jewish community in Iran has remained uninterrupted, though often endangered, to this day.

This is the story of the dramatic liberation of Iranian Jewry from a cutthroat revolutionary regime that today threatens not only Israel and the Jewish people, but the entire civilized world.

The plan began to take shape in conversations at my home in Forest Hills, New York with a young rabbinical student of Iranian descent named Hertzel Illulian. Hertzel shared with us a compelling depiction of the state of affairs in his ancestral homeland. The Shah had given the Jews equality, he explained, and they had advanced in areas of science, medicine, technology, and business. It appeared that the Jewish future in modern Iran was filled with good fortune and great opportunities. On the other hand, when it came to religious observance and Torah study, Hertzel realized that Jewish life in Iran had deteriorated terribly. Under those circumstances, he felt that *now* was just the right time for a special mission to reach out to his "brothers and sisters" in Iran, with opportunities to strengthen Torah observance. We debated, and argued, and finally we resolved together to do whatever possible to enhance the Persian Jewish reality and strengthen Jewish observance in the Iranian Jewish community. With this in mind, and with the blessing of the Lubavitcher Rebbe, Hertzel and I travelled to Iran in August of 1978.

During our stay, the initial stages of the Iranian revolution were playing out on the streets of Tehran. This led us to the awakening that the Jewish community of Iran was increasingly susceptible to threats of an as-yet uncertain nature. Upon returning to New York we were determined to seek ways of assisting the Iranian people, reaching out to institutions and individuals who would be in a position to help. It was then that my father, Rabbi Yaakov Yehudah (known as J.J.) Hecht, of blessed memory, under the direction of the Lubavitcher Rebbe of sainted memory, took upon his shoulders the enormous task of arranging the rescue of thousands of Iranian Jewish youths from Iran—an undertaking that would come to be known as *Escape from Iran*.

The full story of the modern exodus of the Jews from Iran has yet to be told. There were several important stages, continuing through the 1980s, in the emigration of the vast majority of the Iranian Jewish community. This book focuses on the first phase of the exodus, primarily students. Some were as young as ten or eleven, others in their late twenties. Some were in elementary school, others in high school, but the vast majority were of college age. Rabbi Hecht helped them flee Iran by providing them with I-20 visas, better known as student visas, so that these young men and women could come to the United States to attend Yeshivot and other appropriate schools.

Because each student has his or her own story, and because there were many devoted activists involved on different levels in various aspects of the program, a complete telling of these remarkable events would require the input of many different people—especially that of the students. There were very committed individuals in Iran who helped arrange for the students to get on the lists, to get their "papers," arrange their travel documents and eventually leave the country. There were others involved in the administration of the Hadar Hatorah Foreign Student Division school here in the United States, who had to take care of all the necessary paperwork. In addition, the administration of Touro College designated a course of study expressly for the Iranian students, in their Manhattan location. There were still others who returned to Iran from America to help in the process. Then there were those who played key roles in England and Italy, including several Chabad emissaries in Rome, Milan and London. Each one of these individuals and institutions involved in this historic enterprise has a different aspect of the story to tell.

Every one of the 3,000 Iranian students who came to America at that time has a unique perspective. So do the young men and women who worked with them in the United States, in the schools, in homes, and in dormitories, encouraging them to put more emphasis on their Torah studies, helping them learn to speak English, and in some cases to improve their Hebrew. The same is true of those who spent the summer months with them in the summer camps, helping them assimilate to the American lifestyle.

The Jewish community in Iran, afraid of the dangerous political events happening around them, did not want to be targeted as traitors. Nor did they want to trigger panic by allowing it to appear that they were actually sending their children away in fear of their lives. But they were! The peril was real. In some areas the threat of violence was palpable on the streets, and women were especially at risk in the fanatically charged political and religious climate. The young men in Iran at that time were being conscripted into the brutal war in Iraq, and Jewish youth were no exception. So despite the reality, when we started bringing the students to America the Iranian Jewish community attempted to assume an attitude of great calm. To some extent they were successful. Most of the children who came to the United States had little idea of the serious threat to their lives and the lives of their families that loomed on the horizon. Some of them believed they were simply going to a boarding school in America. "Ah great! We are going to have a wonderful time!" But with the clear vision of hindsight we can say with certainty that as the Iranian revolution developed, the Jews in Iran would face serious, dangerous anti-Semitism that would jeopardize their very existence.

Initially, it was not a religious revolution. The original demonstrators were students, workers, and democracy activists. Though content, perhaps, with the growing economy of Iran, they were very troubled by the widening gap between the rich and the poor. They hated the authoritarian rule of the Shah. They knew that the Shah's secret police, the Savak, used terrorist methods to accomplish their nefarious ends. So the first wave of rebellion had nothing to do with Islamic Revolution. It was about democracy and seeking independence from the tyranny of the monarchy. At some point the fanatic Islamists saw an opportunity, jumped on the band wagon, threw everyone else off, and took over the revolution. "Like so many revolutions," in the words of respected historian Tim Mackintosh-Smith, "it was begun by those who were hungry for justice, but was hijacked by those who were hungry for power."* Then, when the Ayatollah Khomeini returned in triumph to Iran, it became a full-fledged Islamic revolution. Those who had been fighting for secular democracy were suddenly overwhelmed, pushed to the background,

---

* Arabs: A 3000-Year History of Peoples, Tribes, and Empires, p. 515

and often threatened with all sorts of torture and incarceration. They had to shut their mouths and accept that what they had begun didn't turn out the way they had hoped.

When we met with college students on several occasions in Iran, we might just as well have been meeting with secular American Jewish kids. They dressed like American kids. The boys and the girls spoke like American kids. They had the same interests in their future, in what they were studying in University, and they displayed a fascination with Western culture—the music, the movies, and all its other trappings (as the renowned contemporary scholar Rabbi Adin Steinsaltz characterized it, "money, fun, and chewing gum.")*

At some point in mid-1979, Jews realized that now there really was a far greater danger than before. When two prominent members of the Jewish community, Habib Elghanian and a member of the affluent Beruchim family, were assassinated under the government's pretext that they were Zionist collaborators, it became abundantly clear to the Jews of Tehran that the future was bleak. Today, Iran's 20,000 remaining Jews do not live exclusively in Tehran, rather; they are dispersed among the smaller,

---

* Lecture to Yeshiva University students, 1996.

outlying cities and provinces. Then, the high-profile Jewish community in Tehran was a sword in the eyes of the fanatical Moslems. Some of the Jews of Tehran, who because of their great wealth would never have survived the ongoing Islamic Revolution, got out as quickly as they could. Many of them would have been singled out like Mr. Elghanian and come to the same terrible end. As we now know, many then realized that the salvation of the Jewish community of Persia would require nothing less than an exodus.

There were far-reaching historical ramifications. The Jewish community had been subject to exile, *galut*, in the Babylonian and Persian empires since the destruction of the first Holy Temple and probably even earlier. Nonetheless, during many periods of our history, *galut Bavel* stood out as the predominant center of Jewish life, civilization, and culture. This was certainly so in Talmudic times, and again later in the early middle ages. The presence of the Jews in Iraq and Iran represented a major segment of the worldwide Jewish community, and the largest concentration of Jews in Sephardi countries. Until the late 1800s, the "*Resh galuta*," the Exilarch in Baghdad, was considered the leader of all Sephardic Jewry, whose prominence was recognized and accepted all over the world. The illustrious Ben Ish Chai, who lived until the early twentieth century, was accepted as the last of those great *Roshei galuta* in Baghdad. The Iranian community's continuous history was of enormous significance in a chain of tradition extending back to the times of the first Beit Hamikdash.

Also worthy of note is the connection between the success of Rabbi J.J. Hecht's efforts to bring the students to America and the subsequent emigration of a majority of the Iranian Jewish community, during the following seven or eight years. In bringing the students to the United States, setting them up in schools, providing them with their needs, and helping them assimilate into American culture, language and customs, Rabbi Hecht provided a framework for the rest of the Persian Jewish community. Their parents and relatives felt secure in the knowledge that their kids had comfortably resettled in the United States, which gave them hope that they could do so as well. In the course of the twentieth century many Middle Eastern lands had seen entire Jewish communities, predominantly Sephardic, thrown into exile, forced to flee their homes or summarily evicted from their countries. Very often the Jewish refugees had no idea where they were going, how they would reestablish their lives, or what they would be able to accomplish when they got there. They had only the shirts on their backs when they were accepted as refugees in new countries. With G-d's help and against all odds, many were blessed to be able to put down new roots, settle their families, and rebuild their communities in the far corners of the world.

In the case of the ensuing Iranian exile, because we had been able to bring the Iranian students to America during the years we worked with them, this provided their parents and families—in perception as well as in reality—with the prospect of a safe haven. They recognized that despite the difficulties of preparing for radical transformation and being uprooted from their ancestral homes, they would be able to make the move out of Iran and into the Western world.

The Prophet Isaiah had long ago foreseen that when the Jews leave Bavel, it will be with "*kaspam u'zhavam itam—together with their silver and gold*," with their wealth intact. Whereas for the most part the other Jewish communities that were thrown out of their countries during the twentieth century had no opportunity whatsoever to take their wealth with them, a significant number of Iranian Jews were able to do so, at least to some degree.

More than likely this was due to the fact that they made every effort to take precautions while still in Iran. In the earlier years, in anticipation of the possible overthrow of the Shah, those who could made provisions for the eventual transfer of their wealth to other places, without knowing exactly how, or where, or when. Nonetheless many families were unable to get their possessions out of Iran in time. For these less fortunate refugees, there came a time when it was necessary for families and community groups to raise funds to help them establish themselves in their new homes.

It has been widely reported, though without official confirmation, that the Shah once met with Iranian Jewish leaders and told them that he could no longer guarantee their protection. Those who participated in or witnessed this event were reluctant (and remain so to this day) to discuss the matter, in fear of retribution at the hands of the long arm of the Iranian regime, then and now. Even had he not told them, the writing was on the wall. And so channels were opened, via families who were already out of the country as well as through other means and other places, for some segments of the community to be able to transfer their wealth, and eventually escape themselves.

When the immigrants and refugees from Iran came to the United States, it was therefore not of the utmost priority to set up relief funds for them, as had been the case when the survivors of the Holocaust came to the United States or to Israel after World

War II, or when large numbers of Moroccan Jews emigrated to Israel. The Jews of Iraq had to utterly abandon their possessions when leaving Baghdad; so too, the Egyptian Jews, when they were thrown out of Egypt in 1948, in 1956 and finally again in 1967. In America in 1979 we were able to focus a bit less on dire financial straits and pay more attention to education. Not that it wasn't costly; but from this historical perspective, and in consideration of the socioeconomic factors in play, it clearly appears that the work we did to bring the students to the United States and provide for their needs was important precursor to the ensuing events. Although some Iranian refugees realized that their only route of escape was via Afghanistan or Pakistan, the relatively straightforward transition that characterized the exodus and the emigration of the entire Jewish Iranian community was unprecedented in modern history.

Though it may not have been obvious to the casual observer at the time, this evolving liberation of the Iranian Jewish community had a spiritual aspect as well. Here I believe it's important for us to understand why the Rebbe was adamant from the outset that we should spare no effort in keeping all the children together in Crown Heights. This, despite the fact that there was great difficulty in housing them and in caring for them; and despite the fact that during that first year we did receive proposals from several organizations in other parts of the City, and in other cities around the US, who offered the use of their facilities. We might have been able to house a number of students and arrange for their schooling there. But it would have meant that they would be separated from their brothers and sisters in Crown Heights, and from the Crown Heights community; and we would have had to forfeit our beneficial influence and control.

The Rebbe understood that the Iranian Jewish community had a rich culture, a glorious history, and had been imbued over centuries with a powerful and somewhat chauvinistic identity as Iranian Jews. He also knew that the vast majority of the Jews in Tehran had become assimilated. Not that they were accepting other religious beliefs, G-d forbid, but simply that they had absorbed and were largely engulfed by the secular values and surrounding influence of Tehran. By the time we arrived in 1978, not only had the Jews been living in an increasingly secular society, but the Shah of Iran had also been engaged ever since his appointment in the early 1950s in a very strong effort to further secularize his country as much as possible. He felt that the future of his country depended on stemming the tide of Islamic fundamentalism and bringing his people out of a medieval mindset and into a modern, secular world. At that time the average Muslim in Iran was not especially religious or fervent. During the weeks that I was there I do not remember seeing any women wearing the Chador or Hijab in Tehran. And in the Jewish community the girls and the boys dressed like American teenagers or college students.

So the Rebbe realized that however strong the community was in Tehran, it did not have a structure that included a Torah life as its cultural mainstay. Nor was there a prevailing influence of traditional Torah values regarding the centrality of the Jewish family. Effective rabbinic leadership was not pervasive, and there were precious few institutions of Torah learning—certainly as compared to Jewish communities in Israel, in America, and especially in the Crown Heights, Brooklyn community.

The Rebbe felt strongly that the Persian students should live, initially, in Crown Heights. His reasoning, I believe, was rooted in the fact that it was a modern, Americanized community, where English, not Yiddish, was the *lingua franca*, and yet the basis and the structure of the society was a Torah-based life. The Yeshivot, for both boys and girls, were the center of everything. The synagogues were a very important part of everyday life; and the rabbinic leadership, headed by the Rebbe himself, was one of the most important aspects of life in Crown Heights. He knew that the families in Crown Heights would happily accept the young refugees into their homes and serve as proper mentors. It was a cohesive community that shared a firm belief and trust in the Rebbe as a righteous *tzadik*, as the leader of the community, and a source of wisdom and practical guidance not just for Lubavitch, but for the generation.

The Iranian Jews of old had been steeped in a traditional understanding and deep appreciation of the ways in which Torah life and Torah leadership are the essence and the glue that hold a community together. Some of these sensibilities had eroded over the years. The Rebbe wanted these students to reclaim the core of their heritage.

We can say now, in retrospect—and looking toward the future—that despite all the difficulties and challenges, despite the millions of dollars of debt incurred, and despite the fact that not every individual Iranian boy or girl fit comfortably into the framework we provided for them, it was a goal well met. On the whole, most of the students who eventually left our community, whether after a few months or a few years, had gained a new appreciation for Torah and a true understanding of what a Jewish community should be like. They saw how Torah and the leadership of the *Chachmei Yisrael*, our Torah sages, provide the essence and the substance of what Jewish life is all about. We also see that when their parents came to the United States and settled here, they too adopted these principles into their own communities. Many more families sent their children to Jewish schools in New York than had done so in Tehran. And many more Jewish families became careful about where they bought their meat, more joyously observant of the laws of *kashrut*, *taharat hamishpacha*, and Shabbat, and cultivated a general appreciation for the Torah standards of Jewish life.

As mentioned above, there remain empty spaces in the story that I have only begun to tell in this book. The full story of the Iranian exodus will no doubt be unveiled in all its glorious detail as others—students, parents, teachers, advocates and activists—will sit down to their computers and fill in the blanks, each with a unique perspective. As these other stories come to light, I am confident that we will begin to acquire a broader and clearer picture of this very important period of Jewish history. More significantly, perhaps, we will gain the understanding necessary to envision the culmination and fulfillment of the history and destiny of *galut Bavel/ Paras*, as the Jews who still remain in Iran after the great exodus continue to preserve and bring renewed vitality to the remnants of this once-great civilization and the faith embodied therein .

There is a group of people today who are picking up where we left off forty years ago, trying to arrange for emissaries to serve the Jewish community still in Iran. Of course, the circumstances are very different now from what they were then. The community is only one-fifth the size it was before the revolution. Interestingly, there are now several new Torah institutions operating in Iran on a very high level, perhaps even more so than they were forty years ago when there were many more Jews there. Our fervent hope is that they will find the right path and the most effective channels to ensure success, and that they will be able to bring to completion the all-important goals which inspired our earliest visits and ongoing efforts in Iran, which brought about the grand exodus of 1978–79.

*Sholem Ber ben HaRav Yaakov Yehuda Hecht,o.b.m.*

*Forest Hills, New York, July 2019*

# CHAPTER I
## The Road to Tehran
ભજી

*August, 1978: The first thing that strikes you when you turn from the airport onto the highway leading to the hotel in the center of Tehran is the extraordinarily heavy traffic. And another remarkable phenomenon—most of the cars are Cadillacs and Mercedes. What a greeting!*

In 1978, Iran was moving from being a leader of "Third World" nations to joining the "Second World." As head of OPEC, the Organization of Petroleum Exporting Countries, Iran was flexing its economic muscles around the world, and business was booming. But the storm clouds that just a short while before had been merely lingering on the horizon were now hurtling toward downtown Tehran.

At that time, I served as rabbi of the Sephardic Congregation of Queens in Forest Hills, New York. Among our congregants were a number of prominent Persian Jews, including several families who identified as members of the close-knit Mashhadi community. Persian Jews had lived in Mashhad, a province of northeastern Iran, for centuries. In the early nineteenth century, under intense Muslim pressure, they had feigned conversion to Islam while practicing their Jewish traditions in secret. As a result they had developed a uniquely proud culture and strong family ties.

During the 1960s many Mashhadi families emigrated from Iran and set up small communities in Milan, Italy; London, England; and Hamburg, Germany. The Milan community, though predominantly Mashhadi, also included non-Mashhadi Iranians, among them, the Illulian family.

Hertzel Illulian, then a student in the Lubavitch Yeshiva in Brooklyn, frequently came to Queens to visit his Persian uncles who were members of my congregation. My wife and I often invited him into our home, where we made him feel very comfortable. He looked up to my wife, Rebbetzin Channah Hecht, almost as an "adopted" aunt, and we welcomed him as though he were a member of the family. Today, he is a highly respected community Rabbi and Chabad-Lubavitch emissary in Los Angeles. Though he had grown up and attended the local Lubavitch school in Milan, with the encouragement of Rabbi Moshe Lazar, who served as the Rabbi of the Mashhadi community there, he transferred to the Lubavitch Yeshiva in Brooklyn. He had long maintained contact with family members in Iran, and at the time of our story his older brother was living in Tehran and serving as an officer in the Iranian Air Force.

Hertzel had a dream: to visit Iran on a Torah outreach mission as an official emissary of Chabad-Lubavitch, and eventually to work toward establishing an ongoing outreach presence in Iran. He had actually written to the Lubavitcher Rebbe, Rabbi Menachem Mendel Schneerson, about his dream, asking for his blessing and guidance. Up to that point in time the Rebbe had not responded.

Interestingly, several months earlier I had met with a Rabbi Tzvi Simantov, a leader of the Afghani community in Israel who had very close friendships with many members of my congregation. He would often come to the United States seeking support for various outreach projects in which he was involved, in Israel, America, and elsewhere. This time he was trying to find young couples who would move to

Iran to be part of a proposed Kollel, a full-time study program that he was hoping to set up. He told me that he had funds available for the project. At that time the state of Jewish observance in Iran was sadly not up to par, which I later witnessed myself when I went to Iran. I inquired as to whether he felt that Lubavitcher young couples could fit into this plan, and he said, absolutely! He would be very happy if the Rebbe would take an interest, support the Kollel, and send couples there; he was certain that would prove very productive.

He also told me that he planned to contact Torah U'Mesorah, the national network of Hebrew Day Schools in the US, to see if they could find appropriate young couples to go to Iran. After discussing this with him in some detail, I wrote a letter to the Rebbe asking for advice as to whether or not to participate in this and continue conversations with him. The Rebbe's answer to me was not to get involved in something that might create competition with Torah U'Mesorah. So at that point, the idea of sending Lubavitchers to Iran seemed to be off the table. As it happened, Rabbi Simantov's plan never got off the ground due to the political changes unfolding in Iran.

Meanwhile Hertzel's dream remained very much alive. In June of 1978 the Rebbe's senior Secretary,

Rabbi Hodakov, advised him to present the idea to me. Hertzel now came to me with a challenging suggestion, that together we should arrange for a *"shlichut"* outreach mission to Iran, under the auspices of *Merkos L'Inyonei Chinuch*, the educational outreach arm of Chabad. *Merkos* oversees a summer program every year, sending young Rabbis to communities around the world to teach and strengthen Jewish practice. He was convinced that this mission would open up opportunities for greatly improving the spiritual quality of Jewish life in Iran. At that time we believed that no official representatives of the Rebbe had visited Iran since 1963.

We later learned that one prominent rabbi had indeed visited Iran in the 1960s and '70s, Rabbi Avraham Mordechai Hershberg—no stranger himself to persecution and exile. Born in Poland, one of the elite students in the legendary Lublin Yeshiva, Rabbi Hershberg was forced to flee when the Nazis invaded Poland, escaping first to Vilna, Lithuania. Luckily, he was among the Jews for whom the legendary Japanese Ambassador to Lithuania issued visas to Japan, rescuing him and many other Jews. From Japan he was sent to the famous (and in many ways infamous) Shanghai Ghetto, along with thousands more refugees. He broke free from Shanghai in the early days of the War and made his way first to Montreal, then to a Rabbinical post in Chicago. From there he emigrated to Mexico, where for twenty-five years he served in close collaboration with his colleague Rabbi Jacob Avigdor, the Chief Rabbi of Mexico and a survivor of Buchenwald. Serving together in a powerful "unaligned" country, they cultivated many contacts among leaders of Arab countries and other world leaders at the United Nations. Consulting frequently with the Lubavitcher Rebbe, he conducted a number of missions to Iran during those years—the last and most dramatic of which was in 1980, during the Iranian hostage crisis. Although this remarkable encounter had some positive impact (see sidebar on the opposite page) and resulted in some temporary leniency on the part of Khomeini and the Islamic Republic of Iran, the safety of the Persian Jews was far from guaranteed. People began to leave Iran in droves to settle in Israel, Europe, and the US.

In 1979, however, no Chabad emissary had been to Iran in many years. Hertzel was determined to step into the breach, and having turned to me, his infectious enthusiasm moved me to partner with him.

I felt it would be helpful to enlist the participation of the American Sefardic/Iranian community, so I approached several members and friends of our congregation in Kew Gardens and Forest Hills. I also reached out to other respected members of the

When the US Embassy in Tehran was overrun by radical Iranian students, holding 52 Americans hostage for 444 days, a United Nations initiative sought Ayatollah Khomeini's permission to bring Christian leaders to Iran to meet with the hostages. Thinking it might be helpful to send a Rabbi as well, they approached Rabbi Hershberg, who then went personally to New York to seek guidance in the matter from the Lubavitcher Rebbe. The Rebbe encouraged him, and further told him to pack a menorah—even though this was in May of 1980, long before the Chanukah holiday. Shortly thereafter Khomeini rescinded his permission, but after a long delay the plan was rescheduled in the Winter. The Rabbi and the Priests were invited to attend a special public religious event being held on Friday, the Muslim holy day. During the prayers, everyone followed the expected protocol, bowing and prostrating themselves at the appropriate time—everyone but Rabbi Hershberg. He was immediately approached by military personnel who demanded to know why he did not bow down. "I only bow down to Hashem," the Rabbi replied. "And not understanding the language, it would have been improper for me to bow without understanding why. I didn't know which words referred to our G-d."

His response was reported to Khomeini, who replied, "we respect you for your honesty and not taking us for fools. You neither flattered nor lied to us." Several days later Khomeini received him in private audience. Rabbi Hershberg discussed with him the plight of the Jews, urging him to show kindness; in the course of their conversation he explained to Khomeini how the blue and white design appearing on a *tallit* (the prayer shawl) has nothing intrinsically to do with the blue and white flag of the "Zionist state"—so no one wearing a *tallit* should be held captive, prosecuted, or harmed. He also came to an understanding with the Ayatollah that Jews found walking to *selichot* services in synagogue at 5 am should not be arrested for violating the curfew.

The menorah did reach the Jewish hostages, who lit the candles that Chanukah.

extended Sephardic community in Queens, including influential Persian émigrés with whom I was friendly. I suggested that it would be very meaningful for these prominent community members, particularly those of Persian descent, to share sponsorship of the proposed trip with Lubavitch. The suggestion was discussed, proposals were presented, and the plan was accepted. We then worked out a strategy to cover all expenses of the trip. Our Iranian friends Mr. Azariah Levy and Mr. Khalil Moradi were among the most generous underwriters.

When we brought this agreement to the attention of Rabbi Hodakov of the Rebbe's Secretariat (he was also the director of the Merkos outreach program), he in turn brought it to the attention of the Rebbe.

At one point while we were discussing the mission to Iran with Rabbi Hodakov, I wrote a letter to the Rebbe informing him of the progress we had made, asking whether or not to go to Iran and beseeching the Rebbe's blessing. The note I wrote to the Rebbe, in English, included the following points:

"When the possibility of *Merkos Shlichut* to Iran arose, I spoke with several businessmen and professionals from Iran, and they agreed to share in the expenses. A meeting with leaders of the Iranian community will be held on Monday, the

26th of Tammuz (in the year 1978) to discuss in detail how they can help the mission.

"I also informed Rabbi Hodakov that I am personally able be one of the *shluchim*, and he has accepted my offer."

After stating several other aspects of the plan, I concluded the letter by asking for the directive of the Rebbe as to whether it was appropriate to go. The answer the Rebbe gave was bilingual: "*Al pi zeh*," (according to what you have written,) "*to go*." And he added, "*Azkir Al HaTzion*," which means that he will mention (i.e. pray for) the mission at the resting place of his father-in-law, the Previous Rebbe. This was the Rebbe's characteristic way of affirming his blessing.

So we had a green light from the Rebbe for the mission, and I personally had a clear blessing that I should be among the people going to Iran. This started the ball rolling and gave purpose and direction to the whole operation of the exodus from Iran.

My plan was to remain in Iran for two weeks. Hertzel's intention was to stay on for an additional two weeks, during which time he'd be joined by our friend Rabbi Yossi Raichik A"H, who was in Israel at the time, and who was already well known as an international travelling ambassador for Chabad. Afterwards they too would return to the United States.

And so, a few days after Tisha B'Av, 1978 (the traditional fast day commemorating the tragic destruction of the Holy Temple in Jerusalem) Hertzel Illulian and I set forth on our flight to Tehran. We had a clear sense of the significance of the mission we were about to undertake; and we had begun to sense the magnanimous hand of Divine Providence guiding our every move. However the magnitude of the historic eruption that would soon occur, and the intensity of the events that lay ahead, remained for the moment beyond our imagination.

# CHAPTER II
## Antiquity & Modernity:
## A New Jew in Tehran
ᏨᏯᎤ

*In 1971 the Shah of Iran, Reza Pahlavi, held
a grand national celebration to which he
invited the Kings, Queens, Presidents, and
Prime Ministers of the nations of the world.
It took place at the ancient Persian capital of
Persepolis, the burial place of Cyrus the Great,
complete with elaborate fireworks, a massive
parade of soldiers garbed in antique uniforms,
and a spectacular sound and light show. His
intention was twofold: to show that although
Iran had embraced modernity and was no
longer stuck in the past, it remained faithful to
its age-old traditions. Ironically, the event also*

*bore an unspoken dual message for the Iranian
Jewish community.*

**M**odern Iran, formerly Persia, was in ancient
times a center of power in the Middle East,
along with Babylonia and Medea. These three king-
doms, known in the Biblical and Talmudic literature
as *Bavel, Paras, u'Madai*, became the seat of Jewish
Diaspora after the destruction of the first Holy Temple in Jerusalem, more than twenty-five centuries
ago. This was the beginning of the history of the
Jewish community of Iran, dramatically portrayed
in the books of Esther, Daniel, Ezra, and Nechemiah.

The area was also the epicenter of Torah learning, until the completion of the Babylonian Talmud
more than a thousand years later. In ancient Persia
and Babylon, Jews—the "People of the Book"—were
respected for their scholarship and exemplary lifestyle, enjoying equal standing and religious freedom.

That began to change with the advent of Islamic
control throughout the Middle East. From the eighth
century onward, non-Muslims came to be considered second-class citizens. During certain historic
periods, the Jews of Persia were treated slightly
better than those in other Arab countries, but generally speaking they were merely "tolerated," given
only a minimal amount of freedom if they did not

convert to Islam. Some non-Muslims under Islamic rule were known as *"dhimmis."* In exchange for the loss of their dignity and liberty, *dhimmis* were afforded some limited protection, but were still generally excluded from holding public office, denied the right to practice many professions or attain high positions, and given only the most degrading jobs. According to the Koran, for example, if a Jew or Christian touches food, it is considered unclean, inedible for Muslims. But they were always subject to the whims and caprices of the local religious or political leaders, including exorbitant taxation, extortion, blackmail, and beatings. The actual extent of the oppression varied, depending on the individual *mullahs* and rulers. In the few centuries leading up to the twentieth century, Jews in all the Iranian cities were made to live in Jewish ghettos, which were called the *"Mahaleh."*

This was true right up until 1953, when under US influence, the previous regime was deposed, and Mohammad Reza Shah Pahlavi was reinstalled as the ruler of Iran. The Swiss-educated Pahlavi brought a new, modern vision to his position. His intention was to develop and bring Iran into the twentieth century, to diminish the reactionary influence of Islam, and to build up the infrastructure of his country with the billions earned from oil money.

Despite his absolute authoritarian control of his country, the new Shah had very progressive ideas. He became an important leader in the world of the Non-Aligned Nations and was a source of new development in the Middle East—and a new partnership with the State of Israel. He also realized early on that the Jews would be faithful and loyal to him, and had the ability to help him develop the economy and Iranian society. For that reason, he became a secret patron of the Jews of Iran. He granted them greater freedom of education and freedom of movement in the cities. He allowed them to buy homes outside of the ghettos, and he permitted them to practice their religion and to build synagogues and Hebrew schools. Although it was only to a limited degree, the Shah did serve to facilitate the development and growth of the Jewish community in Iran, and as a result the Jews prospered and thrived more than they had for centuries.

As their independence and self-sufficiency expanded, however, the Jews of Iran also realized that they could not rely on these newfound freedoms. As time went on this became more and more apparent. In fact there is reliable evidence to the effect that years later, not long before the Khomeini revolution, the Shah himself secretly met with some Jewish leaders, told them he could no longer guarantee their future, and suggested that they should make contingency plans. And so they did, as we shall see.

Of more immediate significance in those early years of Shah Pahlavi's reign was the fact that with these new freedoms came a certain amount of cultural assimilation. Religious assimilation per se was virtually non-existent, and there was no intermarriage, but the generally advancing secular trends in Iranian society became increasingly influential within the Jewish community as well. Iranian Jews were still excluded from high societal, government and military positions; nevertheless, Jews were now able to have prosperous businesses through their good connections. These included not only their traditional roles in commerce, such as import-export, retail sales, and carpet stores, but also in the oil business, and professional positions in education, engineering, law, and medicine. By 1978, ten percent of the doctors in Tehran were Jewish. Inevitably, the cultural assimilation and secularism that accompanied these inroads into mainstream Iranian society also had a negative effect on the level of religious Jewish observance.

When Hertzel Illulian and I arrived in Tehran in August of 1978, a major item on our agenda was to assess the state of Jewish education and its impact on the lives of the Jewish community Clearly, there had been a lack of *Hachamim*—Torah scholars who had been trained in Iran and were conversant with the orientation and needs of the Iranian Jews. Over the years, therefore, Torah study in Iran had diminished greatly.

At first we met with people who were connected with an educational organization called Otzar HaTorah. This was a network of schools that had been set up around the time of the Second World War by Rabbi Yitzchok Meir Levy, a European educator who had come to Iran and realized that the Iranian community did not yet have a proper Yeshiva system in place. Rabbi Levy began by establishing the Otzar HaTorah school system, in the hope that it would eventually develop into a full-fledged institution. It was successful for a while. At one point, there were over eight thousand students enrolled in the various divisions of Otzar Hatorah. But the advancing secularization that followed with the new regime took its toll, and by the time we arrived in 1978, there were only three hundred pupils enrolled in Tehran.

We met with HaRav Netanel Ben-Haim, the head of Otzar HaTorah at the time. He was a very respected, elderly rabbi who had also studied in Rishon Letzion, Israel, and was held in high esteem among the entire Iranian community. The rabbi's wife was the sister of HaRav Mordechai Eliyahu, of blessed memory, later the Chief Rabbi of Israel. There was also an American rabbi, who had been appointed by the international office of Otzar HaTorah to serve as executive director of the Otzar HaTorah School system. We consulted with him as well during our stay there, and had several extensive meetings with the Directors, to explore in detail how the schools could once again grow and attract more students.

But though these efforts on the institutional level were of great importance, we recognized a pressing need to reach out more directly to the people.

# CHAPTER III

## Shul Hopping, Persian Style

ભળ

A "maggid"—an itinerant preacher—is addressing the crowd in an unfamiliar synagogue. He notices an elderly gentleman in the front row, grimacing, gesticulating, shaking his head, first up and down, then right to left. After the sermon he approaches the old man and inquires, "what was it in my speech that seemed to inspire you so intensely?"

"I lost a goat last week," the man replies. "At first you reminded me of my goat. Then I thought, nu, so maybe he's not really a goat."

"What did you decide in the end?"

"A goat you are," he says. "But you're not my goat."

During the time I was in Iran, we made arrangements to speak in various synagogues, and worked out our schedule so that during my initial two week stay we'd be able to visit the five largest Shuls in Tehran.

One of these Shuls was considered the preeminent *Beit Knesset* in the city, at the center of the Jewish community: the Abrishami Synagogue. Approaching the place, we were surprised to find a nondescript building with plain white stucco walls, large supporting pillars on the ground floor, and except for the name, no external signs that made it look like a Shul at all. It might as well have been a large warehouse; there was no structural evidence that this was a house of worship. The actual sanctuary was up a rough-hewn staircase on the second floor of the building, again, reminiscent of a warehouse loft. It too was of the utmost simplicity, devoid of any elaborate décor or color or aesthetic design. But what it lacked in beauty, it made up for in functional space. There were seats for about 1,500 people, chairs and benches that filled the room, a *mechitza* curtain demarcating the women's section, a *bima* table in the center, and an unadorned *Aron Kodesh* (the Holy Ark that housed the Torah scrolls) in front.

This was clearly the largest Shul in Iran. It was the synagogue where the Chief Rabbi of Tehran, Rabbi Yedidia Shofet, would pray, and he served there as the pulpit Rabbi. But no overt place of honor had been designated for him. He sat on a chair in a row near the *bima*, facing the front of the room like everyone else, and nearby sat his son, Rabbi David Shofet.

Years before, at his father's request, Rabbi David had traveled to America, where he studied in Yeshiva and enrolled in various Torah study centers. Now he was back in Tehran. Upon our arrival, we had been advised to meet with the leadership of the *Anjoman*, the Jewish Committee, Rabbi David Shofet among them. The scion of twelve generations of distinguished rabbis, he received us with a great deal of respect and interest. None of us could then know that in a matter of a few years he would find himself in an altogether different environment, as the founding Rabbi of an affluent Iranian Jewish Center in Beverly Hills, California. But that would be then; this was now. We remained in constant contact with him throughout our stay.

The Abrishami Synagogue had a microphone and amplifier system. Ordinarily, according to mainstream Orthodox standards, this is not permitted for use on Sabbaths and Festivals. Here, however, they felt that it was allowed for the Chazzan and the Rabbi to utilize amplification on Shabbat, based on certain leniencies which they felt existed within the guidelines of *Halacha*, Jewish Law.

I was invited to speak at the Abrishami Synagogue on the first Friday night that we were in Iran. In Tehran, Friday night was when most of the people came to Shul. Friday is the holiest day of the week and the day of rest in the Muslim religion, and therefore all businesses are closed on Friday, and all the Muslims attend services in their Mosques. The Jews were also required to observe the Islamic "Holy Day" and were therefore off from work on Fridays. By going to Shul on Friday evening, they were in a sense demonstrating a measure of respect toward their Muslim neighbors. On Saturday mornings there were fewer people at Shul, but some of the synagogues did still have relatively high attendance on Shabbat morning.

When I got up to speak and approached the podium, I realized that the microphone was there, although I had been assured that the P.A. system would be turned off. I hesitated for a moment, then took off my hat and placed it over the microphone to indicate clearly that I was not using it.

Before leaving New York, knowing that in all likelihood I'd be called upon to speak, I had asked my father Rabbi Jacob J. Hecht for advice. He guided me well. I began my talk with a Biblical quotation from the story of Joseph and his brothers. Yosef had been separated from his brothers, even somewhat estranged. When they were far away from home, pasturing their flocks, his father Ya'akov sent him on a mission to find them. Confronted by the Angel Gabriel, who inquired as to the nature of his mission, Yosef answered, "*Et achai anochi m'vakesh*—I am seeking my brethren."

This, I explained, was what I too was doing, here in Tehran: I came as a representative of the Persian and Sephardic community in Queens, where I serve as Rabbi, and also as an emissary of the Lubavitcher Rebbe. I told them about the beautiful community of Iranian Jews in Queens, many of whom had become very successful in business, and had generously contributed to the expenses of our trip. Out of love for their brethren, I said, amidst deep and abiding concern for their welfare, they sent me to Tehran to reach out to this community. "We're here to meet our brothers, to see how they live as Jews, to join hands between our two communities, and to explore whatever ways we may be of help to strengthen Jewish life in Iran."

I spoke also about the love the Lubavitcher Rebbe had for Jews everywhere—that even though he was far away in Brooklyn, he was considered a leader of world Jewry who cared about the well-being of every single Jewish person. "The Rebbe has sent us here," I said, as he sends his emissaries around the globe, "to encourage more enthusiastic observance of Torah and Mitzvos—in deepening and expanding the accessibility of Torah learning, in strengthening the existing Jewish educational institutions, in enhancing the quality of Kashruth, and more . . ."

I also made sure to mention that we were not there to raise funds. This was important to clarify, since throughout the years the only rabbis who generally showed up in Iran were those who came to raise money for Yeshivot and other organizations. After this was understood, it created an extra measure of excellent rapport with the people. And in all my subsequent talks in the other synagogues, I expanded on these same themes, and was pleased to see how our presence in Tehran was so deeply appreciated.

The next morning we prayed in the Otzar HaTorah Yeshiva/Shul, a much smaller venue which had seating for about 200 people. It was, however, quite full. Here too there was no elaborate décor—no art or images or even signs, just a simple, rather stark, utilitarian space. But the space was filled with the charming, innocent, youthful spirit of the Yeshiva. I was very impressed with the *Chazzanim* and their cantorial melodies for the morning services, *Shacha-*

*rit* and *Mussaf*. They were all young men—actually teenagers—who were able to read very beautifully and led the various parts of the *davening* and Torah reading. This was clearly due to the dedicated work of Rabbi Netanel Ben-Haim, their teacher and mentor. We would soon get to know him and his family better.

My speech that morning at Otzar HaTorah was in a similar vein to the talk I had given the evening before, with the addition of some appreciative remarks about the school itself. The Lubavitcher Rebbe, I told them, will be delighted to hear our report of the wonderful atmosphere here, and how the young boys especially are able to lead the prayers and read so beautifully . . . and that the Persian Jews in my own community of Queens will no doubt be inspired as well.

When we first arrived in Iran we were inclined to assume that Hertzel Illulian, being an Iranian who spoke a bit of Farsi at home, would be able to serve as our translator to facilitate communication. But when we got there, and he started to translate my talks and conversations into Farsi, the Persian language, people would sometimes stare blankly in response to his efforts, barely able to understand. Some would smile condescendingly when they got what we were saying; it was often frustrating. Those uncertain moments at the podium, wondering what the people were actually thinking, reminded me a bit of the story about the old man in Shul, who couldn't stop imagining during the sermon that the speaker looked like his missing goat.

So we realized that we would need a better interpreter. We were referred to a gentleman whose name was Mr. Abrishami, who had worked as an official translator for the Persian government. Farsi was his native tongue, and he also spoke English beautifully. He graciously volunteered to be our interpreter. So Mr. Abrishami became our official interpreter for the remainder of our stay, and he went along with us wherever we went. Whenever we made official speeches he was always there to translate for us, and we eventually became very close friends. Later, when he emigrated to America, he moved to Queens and became a member of our congregation in Forest Hills. He was a man of the highest integrity and sterling character, a truly wonderful Jew.

On the second Friday night that we were in Tehran we went to the Beit Knesset that was called the Baghé Saba Synagogue, which was a very large and very different sort of Shul. Whereas the Abrishami Beit Knesset had been spread out all on one floor with the women seated behind a simple Mechitza, in the Baghé Saba Shul there was a high ceiling and a balcony. Most of the women were seated up in the balcony, while the men generally prayed downstairs. All told there was seating for perhaps 500 to 600 worshippers. On the night that we were there, however, there was such a large overflow crowd (perhaps due to the word of mouth since the previous Shabbat) that people were standing and sitting everywhere and anywhere they could—in the hallways, in the aisles, and on the stairs. They had gathered to greet and listen to their respected guests, the Rebbe's emissaries, who had come all the way from America to spend some time with them. We felt truly honored; it was a tremendous Kiddush Hashem, a sanctification of G-d's Name.

The Baghé Saba Shul was more like a classical European synagogue than any place we had seen thus far. There were colorfully painted walls and ceiling, and an ornately decorated *Aron Kodesh*. With striking traditional designs gracing the front wall, it was a magnificent structure in the style of the great Shuls of the late nineteenth and early twentieth centuries, in Brooklyn and Manhattan as well as in the European capitals. The beautiful *Bima* in the center, where the Torah was read, had steps leading up to the platform and elaborate wood-carved railings that lent an impressive air of majesty to the entire room.

The following day, Shabbat morning, we were again received very enthusiastically by this community, in yet another venue, when we went to the nearby Yusef Abad Synagogue. It was also known as the Youssian Shul, so named in honor of the major donor, Mr. Youssian, who was largely responsible for both the original establishment and the ongoing upkeep of the building. At the time it was considered the most beautiful Shul in Tehran, and seated over 1,000 people. The room was wider than it was long. It had a very large balcony for the women along the back wall, though when the Shul was full some women also sat in a women's section downstairs, to the side of where the men prayed. There were elegant decorations and beautiful artwork of a more modern style on the front wall and surrounding the *Aron Kodesh*. Colorful mosaics adorned the interior, complete with Scriptural quotations and a magnificent Menorah design incorporating the traditional verses of the 67th Psalm, *Lamenatzeach*.

One could tell from the outside that this was a Shul. There was an eight-foot high wall built all around the courtyard of the Synagogue, for protection, with the very large building set back about ten feet within the wall. Unlike the other Shuls we had seen so far, it was very obvious that this was a Jewish place of worship. There was a sizable crowd that morning, and we were once again honored with the opportunity to address the Congregation.

Rabbi Eliyahu Ben-Haim, the spiritual leader of the Youssian Shul, also served simultaneously as Rabbi, Baal Koreh (Torah Reader) and Hazzan (Cantor) in another synagogue, the Mashhadi Shul. He would pray first on Shabbat mornings in the Youssian Shul and then hurry over to the Mashhadi Shul. It was about a forty-five-minute walk from the Youssian Shul to the Mashhadi Shul. So after my talk, we did not stay there for the *Mussaf* service, but rather accompanied Rabbi Ben-Haim, walking through a bustling downtown transportation hub.

Arriving at the Mashhadi Synagogue, we came upon a very beautiful building. At first glance it appeared to be an office building, six stories high. Looking up, however, we could see stained glass windows along the exterior of the fourth story, where, as we would soon see, the Synagogue itself was located. Climbing the stairs, navigating the hallways past what looked mostly like classrooms, we came to the Shul on the fourth floor and were once again deeply impressed by the opulent, modern interior design. Rich mahogany woodwork lined the walls and served as a setting for beautiful pictures and stained-glass windows depicting the Twelve Tribes, Jewish Festivals, and other evocative images from traditional Jewish lore. And here again, we were welcomed with great respect, as we addressed the Mashhadi crowd. As before, we spoke of the Rebbe, and of the Mashhadi and other Iranian Jewish members of my community in Queens, bringing the Rebbe's message of warmth and love and encouragement in all dimensions of Jewish life.

As I've mentioned in previous chapters and will explore in further depth in chapters to come, the

Next to the Youssian Synagogue was the community Mikvah of Tehran: a beautiful building, housing a stunning, impeccably clean Mikvah. It was very large—in fact the Mikvah was the size of a small swimming pool. We used the Mikvah ourselves on Friday and had a chance to speak with the people in charge. To our surprise and dismay, we were told that only a small number of women actually used the Mikvah on a monthly basis. Inasmuch as this was the main Mikvah of the entire community, it was a serious disappointment to us to realize the level to which observance of *Taharat Hamishpacha*—Family Purity—had fallen. We had already begun to see a similar state of affairs with regard to Kashruth; the urgency of educating and helping to strengthen the Jewish commitment of the people of Iran was becoming abundantly clear.

Mashhadi community has a special history and an unusual, idiosyncratic character among all the various flavors and ethnic sub-groups of Persian Jewry. I had already been well aware of this back in my own community in Queens, where there were many members of Mashhadi origin. But I was beginning to see in Tehran that there was much more to learn, and that the Mashhadi people would have a very unique role to play—not only in the coming exodus of young people from Iran, but also in the establishment of extraordinary new Persian Jewish communities in cities throughout the United States.

# CHAPTER IV
## Living the Lifestyle
ભજી

*One afternoon, on a busy downtown thoroughfare, I saw a Persian merchant leading a donkey loaded with merchandise in the middle of the road. Both he and the donkey seemed oblivious to the steady stream of luxury vehicles zipping back and forth. A brief lull in the traffic revealed a crate of Jaffa oranges, imported from Israel, in front of a fruit shop across the street. At that time Iran had good relations with Israel—a situation that was not likely to last.*

*So many contrasts! Not just between modernity and the old world, but between feelings of security and foreboding.*

In the residential areas of Tehran there were many multiple dwellings and large apartment buildings, but we also saw a lot of single-family homes. The mode of construction in the city was probably closer to European architecture than to the American style. One ubiquitous feature—in the Middle East, this was even more common and more widespread than in Europe—was the presence of walls, nearly everywhere you turned. Virtually every home had a wall built in front of it, between the edge of the property and the sidewalk. Thus, when making your way along an ordinary street in the city that was lined on both sides by private homes, all you would actually see was a continuous row of six- to eight-foot high walls, made of brick, or stone, or solid wood, or any other type of material that the homeowner could afford. This was not only about privacy, though surely that was part of the purpose, but there was clearly some degree of protection and safety intended for the inhabitants of these homes.

Having some sort of garden, or lawn, or maybe a few trees in front of the home seemed to be all but obligatory. Nonetheless the space between the entrance of the house and the sidewalk was completely enclosed by a high solid wall all around the perimeter. The backyards, too, when there was a backyard, were equally protected and surrounded by walls.

Some of the homes we visited were set back from the road with very large areas in front of the house. One particular home where we spent a fair amount of time had a beautiful, large in-ground swimming pool in the front yard. But here too, the entire area was surrounded by a very high solid wall all around so as to provide privacy and protection for both residents and visitors.

This not to say that there was no sense of belonging to a community or a neighborhood. Among the people we got to know there was in fact a strong camaraderie; but it was no doubt cultivated in other ways than in shared spaces. People did not sit out in front of their houses and "schmooze" with next-door or across-the-street neighbors. There was simply no common area for such a thing to take place. You can't easily relate to the houses on the street if all you see is a high wall along the edge of the sidewalk. So the physical environment tended to foster an atmosphere of isolation. Somehow, however, people managed to penetrate the barriers and develop a social milieu. This was certainly true of the Jews we met, but I suspect it was equally true of the non-Jewish population.

For our stay in Tehran we had made arrangements to lodge at the Sinai Hotel, also called the "Royal Gardens," which was owned by the Beruchim family, a Jewish family of hoteliers and educators. (Before too long this lovely family would suffer terribly at the hands of the not-yet foreseeable regime change.) The hotel had two sections: an older building, which appeared to us to be no more than a one-star hotel, and a newer part, considerably more well-appointed, which most likely deserved a four-star rating. Assuming, perhaps, that we were in Iran to collect charity, ("schnorrers" would have been the Yiddish appellation; I'm not sure what the equivalent term is in Farsi) the Beruchim family had put us into the old hotel. We were very uncomfortable there, as it really was very low-class accommodations.

We requested to be transferred. We met with a member of the Beruchim family and explained the "non-fundraising" purpose of our trip, after which they generously invited us to move in to the better section of the hotel. It was an imposing new building of contemporary design, such as might have been seen in any big city in Europe or America. There was a large beautiful lobby, marble floors, several very fancy shops and a restaurant and coffee shop off the lobby. There was an outdoor swimming pool, and the rooms were equipped with air conditioning, heating, televisions, etc. Several times we were able to go up to the roof, from which we enjoyed a spectacular bird's eye view of the city. From that vantage point we were a bit surprised to see many dozens of construction cranes. Tehran was in the midst of a building boom.

And so it was that we settled into the hotel and we began making contact with Iranian citizens. Our first interactions were with the chambermaids who took care of the rooms. Because we wanted to appear polite and gentlemanly, we tried to speak with them using some Persian-style niceties, which afforded me my first experience of learning a few words in Farsi. There was an expression that these simple workers used frequently, which caught my attention right away. The word, usually invoked when saying "goodbye," was "*Khuda hafiz*." It means, "may G-d protect you" or "may G-d be with you." It's a universal term, used by all different sorts of people, and it provides a very refined and uplifting conclusion to a conversation or discussion, or even sometimes of a sentence. Clearly, the general population of Tehran had strong religious leanings, and in their culture the idea of blessing a person with Divinely granted well-being was something of great importance. So I learned my first Persian expression, and it was a good one, "*Khuda hafiz*."

The next Farsi word I learned, interestingly enough, is not Persian at all. Because of the great influence of the French culture in Persian society during the twentieth century, especially since the Shah himself was proficient in French and English, it became common for people to use the word *"merci"* to say "thank you" rather than the Persian word *mamnoon*. So *"merci"* was another word that was frequently heard, commonly used in Iranian discourse to express thanks and appreciation. It lent a somewhat cosmopolitan flavor to casual conversations, an air of international significance.

Actually, as I discovered eventually, the words *Khuda hafiz* are also not purely Persian. Apparently it is a pan-Arabic or pan-Middle-Eastern expression which has been adopted by many different languages. Culturally speaking, this idea of invoking the blessing of G-d is considered very important. In that sense it is similar to the word *"Inshallah,"* which means, "may G-d will it to be." *Inshallah* is also a word that, while clearly of Arabic origin, is found in other Middle Eastern dialects, and it has more recently taken on an international identity, used even in a number of languages outside the Middle East.

So my Iranian vocabulary was expanding. Not all that much—I didn't advance much beyond *Khuda hafiz*, *mamnoon*, and *Inshallah*—but I did also learn to count in Farsi: *yeck*, one; *doh*, two; *seh*, three . . . In any event this gave me a few words to ingratiate myself with the people with whom we were dealing, and helped me to grow more comfortable in my new surroundings.

Once we settled into our new room we felt we were in a much more conducive environment—not just for our own comfort, but because we were now able to receive and meet with the various people we wanted to contact, or who sought us out, during our stay in Tehran. The hotel lobby was large, with a number of relaxed yet businesslike areas where we could sit on armchairs, or couches, or at a table, and speak with our visitors. The ability to have a drink or other refreshments while pursuing purposeful conversations makes for a much more amenable experience.

The floors in the main lobby were constructed of ceramic or marble tiles. This being Iran, all of the stone floors were covered with very large, very beautiful, intricately woven Persian rugs. I found it interesting that the cleaning staff in the hotel would come down every day and roll up the carpets, then mop the stone floors clean. They did not vacuum the carpets in the lobby; they took them out someplace, where, evidently, they were either vacuumed or brushed clean. Then a while later they brought the rugs back in, unrolled them, and put them back in place on the floor. This seemed to me a bit strange. In any other environment I'd seen, they would have just vacuumed the rugs right there on the spot. Apparently this is the traditional way in which Persian rugs and floors are cleaned. It's of no great consequence, of course, just one of those small cultural nuances that adds to the fascination of spending time in a faraway land among people of different sensibilities.

We actually felt quite comfortable during the weeks we were there in Tehran. Though this was certainly not the case throughout the city, the areas in which we spent most of our time were sufficiently up-to-date to suit our Western temperament, yet exotic enough to pique our interest at every turn. Most of our dealings were in the business district or nearby, between the hotel, the major synagogues, and the office of the Jewish *Anjoman*, the Jewish Community Council. The traffic on the roads was heavy and sometimes intimidating, but manageable, or even amusing (see Chapter VI); and our occasional walking tours through the streets of Tehran opened our eyes to fresh, diverse lifestyles, as well as to the old-world charms and the dynamic changes unfolding in the new Middle East.

During the week we made a special effort to visit the Jewish hospital in Tehran. We were actually sort of happy to see that there was such a thing as a Jewish hospital. It was in the old Jewish ghetto area, where the entire community had once been concentrated, before the advent of the more relaxed, liberal regime of the current Shah. There were Jewish doctors, and Jewish nurses, and there was Hebrew lettering everywhere. We visited patients, put on Tefillin with several of the doctors and patients, and spoke words of encouragement to whomever we met. It was a very interesting, and in its own small way, productive visit. While there we also took advantage of the opportunity to visit several of the old synagogues in the ghetto district, the *Mahaleh* district, where the Jews used to live. There were some Jews still living there; they still maintained their small Shuls, and there were even one or two Mikvahs in the area. We were heartened by the possibility that in those neighborhoods these Mikvahs may have been used more regularly than the large, modern, underused Mikvah at the big Synagogue on the new side of town.

Being that we were in a Middle Eastern country with ancient roots, we suspected that we might come across the old-style communal bread-baking ovens on the shopping streets. We were not disappointed. We watched with great interest as the dough was first rolled out to about the size of a pizza, but a bit thicker, and then placed on a round "pillow." This dough was then smacked against the inside wall of the ball-shaped oven, which looked like a giant ceramic vat, where it stuck on the walls facing the fire just as described in the Babylonian Talmud. "*Hidbik pat b'tanur*," the Talmud explains—"they stuck the bread to the oven." The old Shuls in the ghetto also had separate ovens in the courtyards where they baked matzo for Pesach.

We also made a point of calling on various people in their homes or offices. Whenever an opportunity arose, such as a Yahrtzeit/Azkara observance or other family event, we would be sure to join other community members in visiting people in their homes. There were some houses I saw in Tehran which were really much more opulent than anything I had seen in the United States, with swimming pools in the front or back yards, and every imaginable modern appliance. We were very impressed by the beauty and the wealth; in fact, some of the latest devices that had been imported to Tehran from Europe had not yet even reached the shores of America in 1978.

One particular visit was to bear fruit for a long time to come. We went to see a wonderful family who ran a very tasteful jewelry shop called *Menora*, on one of the major commercial streets in Tehran. I remember the name of the street to this day: "*Takhh-e-Jamshid.*" The proprietor, Mr. David Kesherim, became very active in helping us work with the community. He was actually a relatively religious fellow, more observant than the average person we met in Iran. We did some business with him there, and eventually he came to the United States and settled in California. His brothers were involved in a number of Torah projects in the US. This was but one of many instances of the links we had the great merit to help initiate between the life that once was in Iran, and the establishment of new Iranian Jewish outposts across the seas.

# CHAPTER V
## Community Roots
☙

*Facing the horrors of the Inquisition in fifteenth Century Spain, the Jews who had been unable to flee went underground, living as Anusim— Marranos—secretly observing Jewish Law and custom while pretending to convert. In nineteenth Century Persia, many Jews chose a similar path, feigning conversion to Islam at the point of a sword. Due to the absence of overt idolatry in the Muslim faith, as well as Islamic dietary laws, it may have been easier to appear to live like a Muslim in Persia rather than as a Catholic in Spain. Nonetheless, in some circles, stealth, secrecy, and a fierce devotion to loyalty became embedded in the Iranian Jewish character and way of life.*

It's been estimated that in 1978 there were a little over 100,000 Jews living in Iran. Most of them probably lived in Tehran, which meant that there were probably 90,000 Jews living in Tehran at the time. Considering that this was a city of several million people, the percentage of the Jewish population was not great. Still, it constituted a pretty large minority. The Jews had long been recognized as being a protected minority in Muslim religious terms. Depending on the time and place, however, the nature of this "protection" was subject to many different interpretations over the centuries. Some of those interpretations turned out to be rather brutal. In any event, by the time we arrived the presence of the Jewish people in Tehran was very visible, well established, and therefore the various Jewish communities were well organized. Unlike the way it was during many other periods in Persian history, there was no need to hide.

This was particularly the case in that the Shah afforded special attention to the Jews. He recognized that they were loyal to him; in fact they very often went out of their way to demonstrate their allegiance to the Shah. In turn, the Shah gave Jews special and unprecedented opportunities to be able to earn their livelihood. It was generally a win-win arrangement—while making money for themselves, at the same time their dealings always managed in some way to add to the wealth of the Shah himself. Despite the fact that the regime ruled ruthlessly and with an iron hand, there was ample opportunity for the entrepreneur.

In this atmosphere of mutual understanding between the Shah, his close government functionaries, and the Jewish community, some Jews were able to attain an impressive degree of wealth during these years. It began in the 1950s and grew more and more profitable into the Sixties and Seventies, as the oil wealth multiplied and was spread around a little more than before. It is difficult to accurately assess what percentage of the people living in Tehran were well-to-do, how many were upper middle-class, and how many had actually remained poor. Some evaluations of the financial structure put the numbers at 10,000 wealthy Jews, perhaps 20,000 living in relative poverty, and approximately 60,000 in the middle-income range.

Demographics, however, are about more than money. Whenever we speak of Iranian Jews and the Jewish community in Tehran, while they can be considered united in many ways, there are cultural distinctions—some subtle, some profound—between diverse sub-communities. More often than not these differences derive from the cities from which they came: from Shiraz and Isfahan in the south; from Hamedan to the west of Tehran; the Tehranis, of course, who had dwelled in the capital city for generations; and the aforementioned Mashhadis, from the city of Mashhad in the far northeastern corner of Iran, not far from Afghanistan and Turkmenistan. And the particularities of these various groups can be understood, to an extent, on the basis of their relationships with the prevailing Muslim populations in their respective areas.

Islam worldwide is separated into two major groups, Shia Muslims and Sunni Muslims. The division came about originally due to a disagreement as to who should become the leader after the death of Muhammad in 632 C.E. Over the centuries the split has widened, often erupting into fierce enmity. Shia Islam is the dominant ruling authority in Iran. Shia overall tends to be more extreme in certain respects than the Sunni version. Be that as it may, for much of its history Shia seems to have leaned more toward absorbing the local non-Muslims.

Generally, whereas through the centuries there were long stretches of time during which the Jewish people were not singled out to be forced to convert to Islam, there were some places and times when the

Jews did in fact face forced conversion. In 12th Century North Africa, for example, during the time of the Rambam (Maimonides), there was an extremist sect of Islam which put tremendous pressure on the Jewish people to accept the basic tenets and principles of the Islamic religion. In his copious writings on Jewish Law the Rambam discusses what the Jews were and were not permitted to do in order to save their lives under those conditions.

More modern times saw many fluctuations between persecution and relative peace. In Iran in the late 1700s and early 1800s, the Jewish community came under severe anti-Semitic oppression. Shiraz was among the cities most susceptible to terrible persecutions in the nineteenth Century; significant numbers of Shirazi Jews submitted to forced conversions to Islam. Many were subjected to intense missionary activity on the part of Christians and the Bahai movement, and many others emigrated to Israel. As late as 1910 there was a blood libel there, accusing the Jews of the ritual murder of a Muslim girl, and the Jewish quarter of Shiraz was mercilessly attacked.

The Islamic persecution in Mashhad came to a head in a blood libel in 1839, after a Jewish woman suffering from a certain malady was told to use dog's blood as one of the ingredients in her remedy. This became the pretext for a mob under the influence of extreme Muslim leaders to slaughter nearly forty Jews in a vicious pogrom. The Mashhadi synagogue was also burned to the ground in the same incident. The remainder of the Jewish community was given a simple choice: conversion, or death.

At that time the community of Mashhad had been isolated for many years, effectively cut off from rest of the Iranian Jews who lived in other areas. When this sudden challenge arose, agonizing over the terrible decision they faced, they turned to the sage leadership of their local *chachamim*, and gazed deeply into their own hearts and souls. What would be the right approach—to submit to the sword, or to survive? The leaders felt the only way to save the population was to appear to accept Islam. As a close-knit community, they came together to the painful conclusion that just as the Jews in Spain had taken on the role of *anusim* centuries before during the Inquisition, they too would hide their observance of Judaism under the guise of outwardly living as Muslims. They called the event, which took place in March of 1839, the *Allahdad*—the "Justice of G-d."

Having undertaken this profound, intense pact of secrecy as a group, the Mashhadi community became bound together to an extraordinary degree, with a fully internalized sense of unshakable loyalty. Each family developed its own strong core of guidelines, rules, and regulations; the entire community knew that the only way they could continue to exist would be if the clandestine nature of their commitment to Judaism was absolute. Virtually no one slipped or strayed from the plan.

Somehow the Mashhadi Jews pulled through. Once they outwardly accepted Islam, they were not persecuted. They had long cultivated a communal sense of unique identity; all the more so now. They continued to keep to themselves, marrying only members of their own community, showing tremendous fidelity to the integrity of their families, and resolute acceptance of parental authority. This became the hallmark of the Mashhadi Jews in Iran.

Over the following century, segments of the community emigrated to Russia, but later returned. Eventually, many families moved to areas where the pressures were eased, and they were able to drop the mask and once again practice the Jewish religion openly. Many of the Mashhadis moved to Afghanistan and Pakistan; more made their way to different areas of Iran, where pockets of Mashhadi Jews settled in and staked their claim. But in every place they retained their sense of solidarity and, to an extent, insularity—as we saw ourselves in our interactions with the Mashhadi Jews of Tehran.

Some were learned, and some were not. But their practical adherence to received tradition was ironclad. The level of observance they took upon themselves became a gold standard that defined them as a cohesive community—so much so that they would frequently resist the efforts of knowledgeable, well-meaning outsiders to mentor them. Any suggestion that they were not doing things the right way or observing the rules properly was met with rejection. Would-be teachers who were not consistent with the traditions to which they had long adhered within their families and closely protected communities were silenced. There were advantages to this sort of lifestyle, as well as disadvantages.

In any case, in the city of Tehran itself, the Mashhadi community developed independently, isolated from the other Iranian Jewish communities. I've already described in Chapter III their beautiful shul building, which contained several floors of offices and classrooms, in addition to the sanctuary itself, with its magnificent stained-glass windows and intricately carved wood trim around the entire room. It seated several hundred people, and attendance was strong. Understandably, perhaps inevitably, their innate loyalty and internal unity led them to also develop a certain suspicion of everyone on the outside. One really had to work hard to gain the trust of the Mashhadis in order to be accepted among them as a teacher, or a Rabbi, or a provider of religious programming and services.

When we visited the Mashhadi community in Iran, our key to acceptance was our long-standing friendship with one of the most respected leaders of the Mashhadi community in Queens, Azariah Levy (who was also among those individuals who had provided financial support for our mission). I had actually helped Mr. Levy in setting up the Mashhadi minyan in Kew Gardens, at the Kew Gardens Synagogue, not far from my own congregation. It was his recommendation that opened the doors in Tehran and enabled me to meet with the leaders of the Mashhadi community there, and to merit an invitation to speak in their Beit Knesset. Later on, once the long and arduous work of bringing thousands of Iranian students to America was well underway, the expatriate Mashhadi community settled predominantly in the Kew Gardens area of Queens. When they were ready to build their own synagogue, I was able to offer some valuable input within their community and grew very close to the leadership.

And it was a symbiotic relationship. When we were setting up schools for the students in Brooklyn (more about that in chapters to come), we realized that Rabbi Eliyahu Ben-Haim, who had hosted us as the Rabbi of the Mashhadi Shul in Tehran, would fit in very well in our program as a teacher for the Iranian students newly arrived in America. During his tenure in Tehran he had actually served two congregations, one of which was the Mashhadi community. We wanted him to come to America and assume his role, once again, as a teacher as well as a Rabbi. So we approached Azariah Levy and the other leaders of the Mashhadis, asking them to partner with us and help arrange for Rabbi Ben-Haim to come to New York.

Over the years in New York, the uniquely chauvinistic attitude of the Mashhadis came to light in several instances. Often, individuals would approach me for advice on various matters, including marriages—particularly when someone from the Mashhadi community was considering marriage to someone who was not a Mashhadi. I had gained a great deal of understanding as to their background, psychology, and frame of reference, as an unwaveringly cohesive group that stands alone and apart. Because of this I was able to offer meaningful advice to those who had turned to me with these pressing questions.

When we had successfully brought many hundreds of Iranian students to the United States, there was a substantial percentage of Mashhadi boys and girls among them. When they did eventually settle in America, they found their way to their fellow Mashhadis, often reuniting with family members who were living in New York or elsewhere in the widespread Iranian diaspora. In Milan, for example, the Iranian community was predominantly Mashhadi. They were proud of the fact that they belonged not merely to a Persian community, but first and foremost to a Mashhadi community. They remained steadfast in their identity and their *minhagim*, their particular customs, in a very diligent and careful fashion. On our part we did our best to accommodate all of the students whom we brought to the United States, always striving to be sensitive to and understanding of their diverse backgrounds and the different customs that the various families followed in Iran.

During our time in Tehran we focused as fully as possible on making every effort to meet with individual people. Sometimes they would come to visit us in the Hotel, and several times we had large groups of people visit us there. That was mostly where we got to know them well. Sometimes we were invited to their homes.

It is customary in the Sephardic communities that during the week of *Shiva*—the seven-day mourning period after the death of a loved one—or perhaps on a *Yahrtzeit*, the yearly anniversary of the passing, a large gathering is held in the home of the family observing the mourning. Sometimes it takes place on the *Shloshim*, at the end of the first thirty days. Very often a meal is served; prayers are recited, and frequently, respected scholars or Rabbis are invited to say a few words of Torah and/or a eulogy in memory of the person who had passed away.

So it was that on one occasion during that first two-week visit to Tehran we were invited to the home of a family observing such a gathering, to memorialize one of their parents who had passed away. We prepared *Divrei Torah*, inspirational talks based on Scriptural passages and Talmudic teachings. Hertzel was to speak first, in Farsi, and I was asked to follow him, speaking in English, with a subsequent translation into Farsi.

Initially we were a bit surprised by the large crowd of people that had gathered there. It soon became evident that this was a truly beautiful, enormous home, with large, spacious dining rooms and living rooms furnished in grand style. As I looked around the home, from the exterior to the interior, I saw many signs of great wealth and opulence in the construction and the design of this magnificent dwelling place. The main living room area where we were seated had intricately carved and beautifully plastered moldings all around the ceilings. There was also a great deal of lavish wooden paneling in different parts of the house. This visit indicated to us that many Jews within the framework of Iranian life, under the patronage of the Shah of Iran, had attained a very pleasant and comfortable level of wealth.

We spoke our words of Torah, and joined together in the prayers, and were genuinely grateful for the opportunity to participate—to share together with this family the heartfelt experience of paying loving respect to their departed parent and grandparent.

Thus, we were encouraged to get together with the many local citizens of the Jewish community, not just speaking formally as Rabbinical figures, but also in more casual, yet meaningful conversation. Hebrew was a familiar language for some; others spoke English. I was able to communicate quite comfortably with a goodly number of individuals in the communities we visited. These encounters proved very purposeful. We would speak about some of the plans we'd been formulating, concerning bringing a Shliach, a permanent, full-time emissary, to Tehran. We also began to broach the subject of a program to bring Iranian students to the United States, where they would have the opportunity for greatly enhanced Jewish education, while furthering their secular and professional education as well. And we planted seeds of hope and enthusiasm toward enriching the quality of Jewish life in Iran.

# CHAPTER VI
## Kashruth, Cars, & Coca-Cola
☙

*I've often noticed, while traveling abroad, that the ways of the natives in any given country or culture can be a complete mystery to the tourist.*

*It takes a while to figure out what makes unfamiliar people tick. And it might take considerably longer to get with the program.*

*Tehrani drivers never really stop for red lights.*

*The prevalent attitude seems to be that a red light doesn't mean stop; at best, it means slow down a bit, look around in all directions, and try to be the first guy to grab the right of way.*

*Fortunately we were able to grasp the significance of this early on.*

For the two Sabbaths we spent in Tehran, we were invited to be the guests of Rabbi Netanel Ben-Haim and his gracious *Rabbanit*. In the States, we'd have shown our appreciation for their hospitality by gifting them with a bottle or two of wine, at the very least. Iran being a Muslim country, however, it was illegal to buy or sell wine, so there was no wine available in the market. Rabbi Ben-Haim told us that every week he would buy a few pounds of grapes, squeeze them thoroughly, and make grape juice for himself to use for Kiddush on Friday night. We enjoyed his fresh homemade grape juice immensely.

Rabbi Ben-Haim was also a *shochet*, a ritual slaughterer well-versed in the laws and methods of *Kashruth*. So he *shechted* a number of chickens every week, not only for his own use, but—by his estimation—for about fifteen other families who relied on him to *shecht* and render Kosher the chickens they needed as well.

We began discussing the issue of *shechita* with him, along with other questions relating to *Kashruth*. There was a Jewish-owned catering hall in Tehran that was equipped to provide services for large events. Many families availed themselves of these facilities when arranging a *Simcha* of some sort—a

Bar Mitzvah, a wedding, or perhaps for *Sheva Brachot*, the celebratory feasts the community would hold for a bride and groom during the week following their wedding. To our chagrin, however, we discovered that there was no such thing as a certified Kosher caterer in the entire city of Tehran. If a family wanted to throw a Kosher party or festive event in any of the available halls, even in the Shuls, they would have to roll up their sleeves, take charge of the kitchen, and do the cooking themselves. They'd also have to go to the *shochet* and have him *shecht* the chickens for the meal. For those who cared enough to go to all that trouble, fine. But if one wanted to rely on someone else to do the catering, the best-case scenario was that perhaps the chickens would have been *shechted*, *kashered* and salted appropriately; but there was no guarantee that all the utensils, pots, ovens, or any of the many implements required at the hall would be under any sort of Kosher supervision whatsoever. This was the situation in Tehran at that time.

Investigating further, we learned that (apart from Rabbi Ben-Haim's fifteen families) there were others who were concerned on a regular basis with acquiring kosher meat. Apparently there were several other *shochtim* in the *Bazaar*, the public marketplace, who were responsible for providing kosher chickens. We went to visit the *Bazaar* and met the *schochet* on duty that day. We were shocked to discover the standards this *shochet* observed. The knife did not measure up to the proper criteria; and they were plucking the chickens with hot water immediately after the *shechita*—also inappropriate. This was the situation for the people who were sincere enough to turn to the *schochet* for the chickens they needed. For others, those who simply went to buy meat in the Kosher store, there was no such thing as trustworthy, well-supervised kosher *shechita* which could be relied upon to provide meat on a regular basis. There were a few kosher butchers who would take the initiative to arrange a *shochet* to *shecht* an animal for them, as had been done throughout Jewish history before the advent of modern *Kashruth* organizations. But their customers were few, and certainly did not number into the tens of thousands that would have been commensurate with the Jewish population of Iran.

Thus, we discovered that there were many, many problems involved with Kashruth. Clearly, the situation in the community was very serious. We began to rack our brains to come up with some suggestions and strategies by which to move forward and resolve these issues. But it seemed the lights had long ago turned red.

Soon after our arrival in Iran we had met a young man named Ben Sion Kohen. He basically showed up one day and offered to volunteer as our chauffeur. He had gotten hold of his father's car, a modest Chevrolet. It wasn't quite on par with the Mercedes Benz 500s or the Cadillac Sevilles that seemed so ubiquitous among the affluent Iranians—there were more Sevilles in Tehran than I'd ever seen even in America!—but we were very pleased to have Ben Sion as our devoted chauffeur in his Chevy. Wherever we had to go, he was always there to take us. He gave us so much time, so much energy, so much dedication, without him we really would not have been able to accomplish much of what we managed to do in the short time we were there. (Ben Sion's devotion did not end there. He remains a good friend to this day.)

With such an expert driver behind the wheel, we had a bit of an opportunity to wax philosophical about the somewhat disconcerting traffic conditions in Tehran. Ben Sion knew instinctively how to navigate these mean streets. There could be waves after waves of cars, three lanes wide, hurtling along, oblivious to the traffic lights. Red lights meant next to nothing to them. And Ben Sion, well-schooled in this environment, would simply forge ahead and take command, yet always remaining alert and cognizant of the other (shall we say) "assertive" drivers competing to take the lead. To a casual observer it may have seemed reckless. But it reminded us of an important truth we had learned in other milieus, in other contexts: with determination and trust in a higher power, obstacles cease to exist.

Before departing on our mission from the United States, I had consulted with several Persian members of my community about the health standards and the availability of Kosher food in Tehran. First and foremost, Aziz Halimi had advised me not to drink the tap water without boiling it, largely because the reservoirs were not reliably cared for and chlorinated. He did say, however, that bottled soda would theoretically be okay. Or so he thought; experience, we found, has a way of debunking the most logical of theories.

As I was pouring my first bottle of Cola into the cup, a strange, fuzzy, sponge-like "thing" floated out together with the soda. I wasn't quite sure whether it was alive, or was merely bouncing around in reactions to the bubbles. In any event that solved the problem of wanting to drink Cola again in Iran. Tea or coffee would have to suffice; having been told to boil the water before drinking, we had brought along a small electric boiling coil and made sure always to boil the water first. We also brought Kosher powdered milk from the States, so we were able to put milk into our coffee or tea.

To meet all contingencies, we had brought along certain Kosher food items which we were told we would not find there: several packages of whole wheat crackers (the ones that were very tightly packed in plastic), a couple of salamis, and a few varieties of hard cheese. We figured fruits and vegetables would be available locally. To our surprise, we did find a few Kosher/Israeli items on the shelves in a supermarket, mostly owing to the still-cordial relationship between Iran and Israel. There was matzo, and tuna from Israel with a proper certification of Kashruth, and quite a few other items. So even if we had not brought supplies with us, we probably would have found enough Kosher food in the supermarkets to survive during the time we were in Iran. But our own survival during this brief trip was beside the point. We were concerned about the sorry state of affairs regarding the awareness of the importance of Kashrut, as well as the overall availability of genuinely kosher food in Iran.

With all the optimism and determination we could muster, we met with the Beruchim family, owners of the Sinai hotel and proprietors of the catering hall mentioned above. The hotel actually had three event halls, and three separate kitchens. We suggested that they designate one kitchen as kosher only. They responded that if we were to provide a qualified person to be the *Mashgiach*, the supervising authority, they would make an effort to set aside one of their kitchens to be koshered and to allow the

*Mashgiach* to guide them in assuring its Kashruth. In that way they would be able to start promoting social affairs with a Kosher kitchen, and begin providing Kosher catering.

So now the availability of a physical venue was potentially there; the next element needed to seal the deal would be to ensure enough demand. We spoke with the leaders of the *Anjoman*, the Jewish Community Committee, and with Rabbi David Shofet, son of the chief Rabbi, about these developments. When we suggested the possibility of providing someone from abroad to coordinate the Kashruth, they assured us that if that proved workable, they would make every effort to summon up the necessary support from the Jewish community—in arranging for the *shochetim* and a place for them to work, in providing sufficient Kosher supplies for the catering business, and, most significantly, in nurturing sustained interest throughout the Jewish community.

Around that same time we had a meeting with the head of Otzar HaTorah about shoring up the quality and quantity of Jewish curricula and classes, in their own schools as well as in other institutions. He told us that if we could send a dynamic and talented emissary to Iran, he was prepared to employ him for half a day, each school day.

An idea began to take shape: if we were to find the right person and come up with the means to send him to Iran, he could work half a day in Jewish education, and half a day in Kashruth. The raising of consciousness on the educational front would stoke the fires of enthusiasm for greater observance in Jewish life; and the increasing availability of kosher food would nourish the clarity of mind it takes to grow in the study of Torah.

But how would we get there from here?

We left the meeting and headed back out onto the street, where the non-stop stream of cars was flowing with its usual reckless abandon, making it nearly impossible to cross over to where Ben Sion was waiting in his Chevy. It was then that we experienced another characteristic Tehran traffic phenomenon: a driver who needed to turn around stopped abruptly and made a U-turn right in the middle of the road, paying hardly any attention to the oncoming cars. Without warning, he spun around and swung across the street facing the other way. Suddenly, the traffic in both directions came to a screeching halt, to allow him to make his U-turn. Nobody moved. In that frozen moment, we were able to take advantage of the unexpected stillness and walk calmly and safely across the street.

Everything that happens, happens for a reason. Though it wasn't all that apparent yet on the surface, Iran at that moment was hurtling from general malaise and unrest toward revolution and regime change—like a sudden U-turn on a national scale. We didn't know quite what it would look like, but an opening was on the way. The time was ripe.

The idea that had dawned on us, to seek and send an emissary from the US to Iran who would become an effective agent of change in Kashruth and Jewish education, began to solidify in our minds. As we entered the last phase of our initial mission to Tehran, this became our emerging plan and goal.

The Abrishami Shul, the Great Synagogue of Tehran

The entrance to the Bagh'saba Synagogue

TOP: The Aron Kodesh of the Yousef'abad Synagogue, with its intricate mosaic Menorah ornamentation

ABOVE: The Ezrat Nashim of the Yusef Abad Synagogue

LEFT: Shiviti Hashem and Aseret HaDibrot in the Yusef Abad Synagogue

ABOVE: In the Jewish hospital of the Tehran Jewish ghetto, putting on Tefillin with a Doctor

LEFT: Herzel Illulian and Rabbi Sholem Ber Hecht in Azadi Square, near the Shahyad Memorial Tower, with the Alborz Mountains in the background

ABOVE AND RIGHT: Ancient portage in modern times, on the commercial streets of the Tehran business district

**ABOVE LEFT:** A young Iranian new arrival in New York

**ABOVE RIGHT:** Hertzel Illulian directing arriving students through the Pan Am Terminal at JFK Airport

**RIGHT:** Registration of newly arrived students in Rabbi J.J. Hecht's East Flatbush synagogue

**BELOW RIGHT:** Iranian students gather together for a welcoming meal during their registration in Rabbi Hecht's shul

English, Math, and Science classes in the secular studies department of the program. Students featured in these photos include Hersel Davoudi, Reuven Shadrouz, Sohrab Vogdani, Nissan Mohaber, and Meyer Cohen.

ABOVE: At the Congregation Bnei Avraham building in East Flatbush provided by Rabbi Michoel Teitelbaum, students pose with our first teacher of ESL (English as a Second Language), Mrs. Jenny Weil.

BELOW: Lefferts General Hospital

TOP AND ABOVE: The Main Building and the Shul &
Classrooms building at Camp Machaneh Mordechai

TOP LEFT: Yisrael Mehdizadeh and friends pursuing musical extracurricular activities

ABOVE: A Purim party for the students at 770 with Rabbi Hecht as Master of Ceremonies

CENTER LEFT: A winter wonderland at Machaneh Mordechai during Chanukah, 1980

BELOW: Persian students line up to receive *Cos Shel Bracha* from the Lubavitcher Rebbe

TOP LEFT: Joseph Abishour receives a trophy for excellence in sports

CENTER LEFT: David Lullian is awarded a set of *seforim* for excellence in his studies by Yosef Gerlitzky, Division Director at Camp Machane Mordechai

BELOW: Yossi Katzman presents a prize for scholarship at Machaneh Mordechai in the summer of 1979

ABOVE: At the Dedication of the Habib Elghanian Persian Synagogue of Brooklyn. Rabbi Jacob J. Hecht presents the plaque to Mr. Sina Elghanian. Aziz Halimi, Gabriel Aharon and Yehuda Abraham, Cantor Mansour Eliav, Rabbi Moshe Lazar of Milan, and Mr. Sam Malamud look on.

ABOVE: Newly arrived Persian student Benham Ben Makabi celebrates his Bar Mitzvah.

ABOVE: Prayers at Machaneh Mordechai during Chanukah of 1980, with Shlomo Mahgerefteh, Reuven Khushanfar, Farhad Jalilfar, and their teacher and counselor Aryeh Sufrin.

TOP: A Tehran movie theater. The Shah's secularization encouraged the emulation of American culture.

ABOVE: A group of newly arrived students at Rabbi Hecht's shul enjoy their first supper in America.

LEFT: Dancing at the Purim celebration in Rabbi Hecht's Shul, 1979. In the background, Yisrael Mehdizadeh.

TOP: The teachers assisted in serving the meals. Right to left in photo: cousins Avi Nissanian and Avi Nissanian, Aryeh Sufrin, Shabsi Chaiton, Chana Arbelli and her husband, Yosef, the chefs.

ABOVE: Havdala at the Machaneh Mordechai Chanukah retreat, 1980.

CENTER RIGHT: Entrance to the Yousef Abbad Synagogue.

RIGHT: View of the Alborz Mountains from the Hotel.

# CHAPTER VII
## Education & Upheaval
ᏩᎨᏋᎠ

*The chaos that had begun churning during our first trip to Iran in August of 1978 was of several dimensions. On one level, it was political unrest, due to corruption, a volatile economy, and a succession of "expert" finance ministers who got themselves fired, one after another. Then there were the radicalized youth, who risked—and lost—their lives in protest against the brutal excesses of the feared SAVAK Secret Police. But it was Islamic fanaticism that finally shattered Iran. Wild rumors foreshadowed the exiled Imam's return to power. One dark November night, millions of the faithful swarmed in the streets, prancing and howling, swearing they could see the image of Ayatollah Khomeini's face in the moon. Sheer lunacy.*

With our revitalized agenda to upgrade the quality of Jewish education in Iran, we made a special effort to visit as many schools as possible in which Jewish children were enrolled. We focused first on the *École Alliance Israelite Universelle*, a long-established network of schools in many cities throughout the country, with hundreds of students in attendance. The Alliance had been founded in Paris in 1860 as an international Jewish organization to safeguard the human rights and self-defense of Jews around the world. The first Alliance school in Iran opened its doors in Tehran in 1898. Known also as the *Etehad* school, it was like a Jewish prep school. Most of the classes were conducted in French, and the curriculum was predominantly devoted to secular subjects, with a very high standard of achievement.

The standards we saw in the relatively small Judaic studies departments were not nearly so rigorous. Not more than an hour or two of Torah or traditional Jewish subjects were offered during any given week. We encouraged the Principal to increase and upgrade the Jewish content of the curriculum. He was sympathetic, if not overly enthusiastic, and he assured us that if the emissary we were planning to send to Iran proved to be a good teacher, as well as available according to the requirements of the school schedule, they would consider hiring him to teach more Torah classes.

The most prominent Torah schools in Tehran were the *Otzar HaTorah* network. It was founded after World War II by Rabbi Isaac Meir Levi, who had come to Iran from eastern Europe for the express purpose of advancing Jewish education. It once boasted, in its early years, thousands of Jewish students all over the country. By the time we arrived, the branch in Tehran had perhaps a few hundred children enrolled. We visited there and spoke with the children. We were most impressed with their sincerity and charm, as we had been the Shabbat before when we saw the children leading the services in the Synagogue. We met also with the teachers, including Rabbi Eliyahu Ben-Haim, who in addition to his responsibilities at the Yusef Abad and Mashhadi Shuls was also teaching there. Of course we also continued our ongoing conversation with his uncle, Rabbi Netanel Ben-Haim, who was in charge or the Otzar Hatorah school and who had welcomed us into his modest home for Shabbat. We arrived at a consensus that there was indeed a great need for more and better educational opportunities and programming in Tehran, not only at Otzar HaTorah, but especially in other Jewish schools which did not have sufficient Jewish curricula. The idea that had already begun take hold in our minds—that of arranging for a qualified emissary to Iran who would be able to devote at least half a day, every day, to Jewish education—became more concrete.

As it happened, at that time there were some friends from our community in Queens on business in Tehran—among them, Hertzel's uncle Mr. Ebrahim Rashtian, and a young man named Habib Lebtob. We were reminded of the dynamic flow of commerce between Queens and Tehran, and by the same token we were comforted by their familiar faces during this critical phase of our mission.

It was our understanding that Hacham Netanel Ben-Haim ("Hacham" is an honorific that means "the Sage," bestowed upon the wisest leaders) did not have any children of his own in Iran. Certainly, however, all the children who studied in Otzar HaTorah Schools at that time, and all those who were a part of Otzar HaTorah Synagogue community, were his children. Being that they were his students and his disciples, they were truly beloved as though they were his own.

Though we could not have foreseen it at the time, Hacham Eliyahu Ben-Haim, his nephew, would soon move back to Eretz Yisrael. As a result of the revolution he retired and resettled there. But for the moment we were only barely cognizant of the explosive events to come. We met with him several times to discuss the various projects that we had in mind, and he made an appointment for us to meet with Mr. Youssian to speak about taking on sponsorship of something along these lines. As a philanthropist, Mr. Youssian was particularly interested in developing something like the after-school programs that are prevalent in the West. It was suggested that the children in secular Iranian schools would be registered in a Talmud Torah, and take classes on Judaic subjects after the end of the regular school day. Although he did not give us a simple "yes" or "no" answer as to whether he was prepared to underwrite our plans, we did discuss with him the programming we had in mind in considerable detail. We felt that there would definitely be a contribution on his part.

Now we had a plan of action. Clearly there was a need for an emissary who would be able to work half a day in Kashruth and half a day in Education. And there was strong potential for local financial support. As we finished up our visit to Tehran, we resolved that upon our return to America we would approach the outreach organizers at Chabad's *Merkos l'Inyanei Chinuch* to report on our findings and the groundwork we had done, and hopefully to begin the search for a candidate for the position.

Events, however, would soon precipitate a significant shift in our plans.

## The Tide Begins to Turn

We had originally intended to visit one or two cities other than Tehran during my two weeks in Iran. But it was at that very time that violent demonstrations against the Shah and his regime had begun to escalate, in various places throughout the country. At first the demonstrators were mostly student activists. It was only later, as the protest movement evolved into a full-scale revolution, that the followers of Khomeini took over.

The Ayatollah Ruhallah Khomeini was a radical Imam who had denounced the Shah and his government and had been exiled from Tehran in 1964. At this time he was living in France, but had many fervent followers in Iran among both the religious leaders and the Islamic rank and file. As the Shah was modernizing Iranian society, distancing it from religion and pushing for a more secularized state, he had not been politically astute. Instead of appeasing and conceding to the Muslim leaders their share in the future of Iranian life, he pressured them in such a way as to make them feel disenfranchised. This was now coming back to haunt him. Because of his dictatorial manner there were many dissatisfied citizens, including previously moderate students and merchants, who turned against the monarchy and began to embrace Islamic fundamentalism. Suddenly there was an awakening among all sorts of people to support Khomeini. While we were in Tehran, demonstrations against the Shah kept popping up; many were violent. We saw them on television, and we were advised not to leave Tehran. We curtailed our planned visits to Jewish communities in other cities, because traveling would likely expose us to danger. Under normal circumstances the Shah's Secret Police, the Savak, would have made sure to quell the unrest. They certainly had the muscle to do so. But for some reason the Shah miscalculated here as well, and did not realize how strong these forces were. Khomeini's charismatic power took virtually everyone by surprise.

As a result of those demonstrations, as we started to realize that this was no passing phenomenon, we began to shift our emphasis from shoring up the educational and Kashruth institutions in Iran, to helping the Jewish population deal with their increasing anxiety. As days went by more and more people sought us out to explore the possibility of sending students from Tehran to New York to study in Yeshiva. During the last few days that I was there we began to make a list of various families who wanted their children to come to America, to be accepted either in a high school or in a college-level program.

These were "interesting times," as they say—an ironic and unstable blend of positive and negative trends. On the one hand we found that the Iranian Jewish community was experiencing a more democratic framework than any other Middle Eastern country. Since the 1950s, Jews had been given the opportunity to attend university, pursue professions, to own and invest in businesses, to attain financial success and benefit from their wealth, and even to be involved with the Shah's government. For the Jews, if not always for the average Iranian citizen—hence the political unrest—the economy was actually booming, with an abundance of opportunity. There were many areas of business in which Jewish people were respected and successful, such as in buying and selling high quality Persian rugs in the *Shuk* (the Bazaar), or other kinds of import/export enterprise.

And yet at the same time it seemed that danger lurked around every corner. Until today it is hard for us to understand exactly how it happened that secular students suddenly became so radicalized, so sympa-

In trying times, it's often the people you meet and the relationships you forge that bring out the deepest meaning. Some of the wonderful friends, residents of Tehran, who helped us immeasurably in our mission and to whom we remain forever indebted, are:

- Rabbi Netanel Ben-Haim, head of Otzar HaTorah, and his Rebbetzin.

- Rabbi Eliyahu Ben-Chaim, spiritual leader of the Youssian and Mashhadi communities, and his Rebbetzin.

- Rabbi David Shofet, head of the *Anjoman*.

- Mr. David Ashuri, one of the exceptional teachers in the Otzar HaTorah School.

- Mr. Abrishami, our translator.

- Ben Sion Kohen, our driver and general helper

- Mr. Kesherim, the jeweler.

- Hertzel Illulian's brother, an officer in the Iranian Air Force; and a number of his cousins, with whom he established a new bond—one of whom subsequently joined the first group of students who came to America.

thetic to those fanatical causes. Why were people so dissatisfied in the presence of such great opportunity? Over the next weeks after we returned to New York, the upheaval and the dominant influence of the religious fanatics utterly transformed life in Iran. Strikes, demonstrations, riots, and mass killings all but crippled the universities, banks, government ministries, oil installations, railways, and bazaars.

The government brought in armed forces to control the demonstrators who had burned banks, gas stations and police stations. On some streets, bullets were flying everywhere. Going out in the street could be fatal.

After a few months, Khomeini returned to Tehran to a hero's welcome, and the Shah was forced to abdicate his throne and flee. Probably one of the strangest twists in the history of the twentieth century.

The Jewish college students we met in Tehran were just beginning to awaken to the turbulence around them. One night we sponsored a gathering for college students, and hundreds came and participated with great interest and enthusiasm. These were secularized Jewish college students, aware of their traditional and family roots in Judaism, but with little formal Jewish education under their belts. They attended various universities in Tehran; it became clear to us that there had been a tremendous surge of academic interaction between Jews and non-Jews in the realm of higher education. Their emphasis was on medicine, on engineering, on science, and numerous other intellectual pursuits. We spoke with them about America, about Israel, about their lives as Jews, and the importance of Jewish observance. Many of them were fascinated by what we had to say. Some expressed interest in the possibility of coming to the United States; others were simply interested in meeting Jews from America.

In retrospect, our interaction with the Jewish college students in Iran turned out to have been among the most significant of our activities there. We didn't foresee it then, but it wasn't long before great numbers of students would come to America, some of whom were among the very students we had met that evening in Tehran, and at other times during our visit. We enjoyed a special relationship with the groups of students who came to New York during the first year of *Escape from Iran*. Many of those warm associations can be traced to these initial encounters.

Shortly thereafter I returned to New York, while Hertzel stayed on in Tehran as we had planned. Soon he was joined by our friend Rabbi Yossi Raichik, something of a world traveler known for his special outreach missions around the globe. He came from

Israel bearing a very precious item—the matrixes with which the printing of special editions of Tanya is accomplished in far-flung locations everywhere. Tanya, the magnum opus of the founder of Chabad, Rabbi Schneur Zalman of Liadi, is the foundational work of Chassidic philosophy. The Rebbe had initiated a global campaign to print new editions of Tanya in hundreds of cities and towns, as a way of linking the centers of civilization with the profound, essential teachings of the inner dimension of Torah. Together with the local Rabbinical leadership, the young Rabbis Raichik and Illulian made the arrangements and (after some delays and difficulties) printed the Tehran edition of Tanya—the 119th edition since the onset of the campaign. Today there are nearly 5,000 such editions worldwide.

There's an amazing story associated with that Tanya. One of Khomeini's first terrible decrees was a "Purification Law" that banned any books with the Shah's royal emblem, or any books published before the advent of Islam. Anyone intentionally harboring such books was in danger of execution. One day the Ayatollah's Religious Police knocked on the door of the Jewish Community Library in Tehran and proceeded to enact the purge. The Rabbi in charge of the Library, the esteemed Persian leader Rabbi Yedidya Ezrahian, was present, and was terrified for his life:

many of the books in the Library were likely to have been among the banned items!

One of the Inspectors spied a box of the newly minted Tanyas near the door, and several copies on one of the tables. Rabbi Ezrahian had planned to send Tanyas to many families in the community. The Inspector picked up a volume. "What is this?" he demanded. "A sacred text of Jewish philosophy," answered Rabbi Ezrahian. The Inspector opened the book. "What does it say here?" He had opened the Tanya to a page in the section entitled *Shaar HaYichud v'HaEmunah*. Rabbi Ezrahian translated what was written there in Hebrew: the mystical teaching that all of Creation, everything that exists, exists only by the immanent power of the Creator, the One G-d of the universe. "If that is the teaching contained in the books of your Library," the Inspector replied, "there is no need for further investigation." He kissed the book, turned, and left. The entire Library, and in all likelihood Rabbi Ezrahian's life, had been saved by the printing of the Tanya.

Meanwhile, as I flew back home to New York—to the Rebbe, and to my family—Hertzel Illulian and Yossi Raichik remained in Tehran and continued to make lists of the families who wished to send their children as students to the United States.

# CHAPTER VIII
## Back Home: Plan B . . . the Exodus Begins
ↂ

*The rescue of the Iranian children was a team effort, to be sure. But above all it was my father, Rabbi Jacob J. Hecht of blessed memory, who shouldered the responsibility—to the extent (to use an expression coined by the Talmudic Sages) of the "wringing out of the soul." The enormous expense and the nonstop self-sacrifice it took to keep the project going was simply overwhelming, and would have stopped any other communal leader. My father's tenacity, unswerving faith in the importance of his mission, and trust in the Rebbe's blessings put him in a league of his own.*

*Late one Friday afternoon, nearly two*
*million dollars in debt and on the brink of*
*despair, my father turned to my brother Rabbi*
*Shea and said, "The Rebbe got me into this. I*
*don't know how we'll get out of it. But if I had*
*to, I'd do it all over again. And if there had to*
*be one thing I did in my life that they'd carve on*
*my headstone, I'd want this to be it."*

By the time I arrived back in the States it had become abundantly clear that we needed a contingency plan. Our original intention, to send an emissary to Iran, was still theoretically on the table; but the demonstrations on the streets of Tehran—nationwide, actually—were becoming more violent and more frequent from day to day. Fear had taken up residence in the hearts of the people, Jews and Muslims alike. The list of students expressing interest in coming to America was growing.

At that time my father was away in Israel. He had gone there for the dedication of a new *Bait HaKnesset* in Jerusalem, where his long-time friend Rabbi Yosef Ralbag, son in law of the well-known Chabad leader Rabbi Azriel Slonim, served as Rav. Rabbi Ralbag and Rabbi Hecht had a friend in common, one of the donors for the construction of the new synagogue in Jerusalem as well as a supporter of my father's organization, the National Committee for the Furtherance of Jewish Education (NCFJE). Although he was out of town, I was able to keep him informed as to the progress of our project; but for the moment at least, the ball was in my court.

The first thing I did in New York was to approach the directors of various established educational institutions, asking whether they would undertake to sponsor Iranian students to come and learn in America. I went to the Lubavitch Yeshivah, under the directorship of the Rebbe's brother in law Rabbi Shmaryahu Gurary, and to Tz'irei Agudas Chabad, the outreach-oriented organization headed by Rabbi Dovid Raskin. I also knocked on the doors of Oholei Torah, the other major Yeshivah in Crown Heights, and Bais Rivkah, the full-service girls' school which, in addition to its large elementary and high school divisions, also ran a seminary for college-age women. What such sponsorship would entail was (beyond the obvious acceptance into the school systems) the issuance of Federal I-20 student visas, and documentation of sufficient financial support. An undertaking of that scale was, at the very least, an excursion into unfamiliar territory. Suffice it to say that the initial responses across the board were somewhat less than enthusiastic.

Seeing that continuing to bang my head against these various walls was not likely to produce the desired result, I put through a call to my father in Jerusalem. Without batting an eye, in his inimitable fashion, Rabbi Hecht said that we'd just have to work together and bring the Iranian kids to America, by hook or by crook. And he immediately went about devising ways in which to do so—some set of as-yet undefined special programs that he would create. He then wrote to the Rebbe for blessings and advice.

The Rebbe replied with a very strong, positive affirmation that included not only blessings for the success of the project, but also assurances that whatever the expense involved (and however counterintuitive it may have seemed) the effort would prove to be beneficial for all the existing programs of his organization as well. To be honest, I don't recall whether Rabbi Hecht wrote this letter while still in Israel, or after his return to New York. But it marked the beginning of a nearly constant stream of back-and-forth communication with the Rebbe about the Iranian situation over the next few years. There was joke going around (actually half in earnest) during those days that there were so many hand-delivered messages flowing to the Rebbe's office at 770 Eastern Parkway from the NCFJE headquarters on the next block, at 824 Eastern Parkway, we should have hired a full-time courier.

One of the flagship institutions under the NCFJE umbrella was the Hadar HaTorah Rabbinical Seminary, the very first Yeshivah in America specifically designed to serve young adults with little or no prior Jewish education. Rabbi Hecht decided immediately to establish the Foreign Student Division of Hadar HaTorah for the Iranian boys. At the same time, he succeeded in convincing Bais Rivkah to work along with him and to accept the girl students. We were therefore able to inform Hertzel Illulian, who was still in Tehran, that it was looking more promising that we'd have places to bring the students when they arrived in the United States. By then, Hertzel's waiting list had grown to about thirty. It was time to start focusing on the paperwork.

The I-20 form, also known informally as a student visa, is the document required by the US State Department, issued by an institution of higher education in the United States, certifying that the named student has been accepted for a course of study in that school. This I-20 is generally valid for up to four years, on the assumption is that it will take somewhere between two and four years for the student to complete the course work in the particular subject for which he or she is enrolled. In our case, we were issuing I-20s for studies in religion, presumably leading toward a Rabbinical ordination. When the I-20 was approved at the US Embassy, the students were issued an F-1 visa, which was the actual student visa.

In addition to the I-20 form listing the course of study, the location of the school, and the auspices under which the person will be studying, it was also necessary to provide a financial support form. Technically, a student who comes to study in the United States must bring a letter of support from the family (or from a financial institution in the home country) indicating that the student will have access to sufficient funds during the time that he or she will be studying in the United States. Alternatively, there could be a sponsor in the United States who promises to take care of the cost of room and board and other personal expenses, for as long as this individual will be staying in America. Under the circumstances, given the unpredictability of access to financial resources in Iran, there was no guarantee that support from home could be provided to the students who would be receiving the I-20s from our organizations. So we decided that it would be necessary to provide them with letters of support confirming local American sponsorship. This meant that the sponsor was assuming responsibility for the room and board of every student given an I-20—an enormous financial commitment. As we began issuing the I-20s and the documents confirming financial support, and as the numbers of students continued to grow, this commitment was to quickly progress into the hundreds of thousands of dollars. The official signatory on both the I-20s and the fiscal documents was none other than my father, Rabbi Jacob J. Hecht.

Upon his return home from Israel, Rabbi Hecht hit the ground running. We began to work at a feverish pace, seeking to establish the appropriate educational and residential structures that would enable us to absorb the students. Shortly thereafter Hertzel came back to America, arriving before Rosh Hashanah, and we began to generate the I-20s and match up to his gradually expanding list of prospective students with the schooling and housing they would require. Once that was underway, we decided that Hertzel would go back to Iran during *Chol HaMoed*, the Intermediate Days of the *Sukkot* festival, with as many of the necessary documents as we could muster in hand. We coordinated with the contacts we had made in Tehran and identified approximately twenty students to join the first group. Some were boys of high school age, several were post-high school, and a few girls were included as well. Rabbi Hecht made initial arrangements to absorb this first cohort in various divisions and different programs under the framework of Hadar HaTorah and Bais Rivka.

Hertzel began packing for his trip back to Iran, and we prepared all the necessary documents for the first twenty students on our list. There was some uncertainty as to whether or not he would have access to a Sukkah there, so we decided to buy a small metal-frame Sukkah with canvas walls, which was about as portable as one could find in those days. We packed it for him to take on the plane, though Pan American Airways was not all that accommodating. This rolled up Sukkah became one of the pieces of luggage he carried with him to Iran. Upon his arrival he immediately set up a system for processing the papers there. The plan was to bring the children to the United States a week or two after Sukkot.

At that moment in time, at the beginning of the month of Tishrei, it was still unclear how many students would eventually request the I-20s. We had managed to arrange placement and housing for the initial twenty students. On the assumption that the numbers would soon rise, we determined that it would probably be possible to make enough room in our dormitory facilities at 824–828 Eastern Parkway to accommodate about one hundred boys. So the plan was to accommodate all of the male students within the framework of Hadar HaTorah, to reside in the dorms and enroll in the Foreign Students Division. The considerably smaller groups of girls could similarly be accommodated within the existing programs of Bais Rivka.

Beyond that, we figured that when it became necessary we would find host families with whom the students could live. In the best-case scenario these families would provide full hospitality; we expected, however, that in some cases the organization would need to undertake to reimburse or cover at least a portion of the expenses. Little did we know at that point how much larger than we had imagined the demand would become.

Over the next few weeks, while Hertzel was processing the paper work in Iran and making arrangements for the first group to leave, the political problem in Iran was rapidly deteriorating. During that time the riots were growing larger and progressively more violent. Hertzel himself was caught up once or twice in very dangerous situations due to his proximity to the disturbances. In one such instance, he happened to be downtown late in the day, near one of Tehran's upscale international hotels. It was time for *Mincha*, the afternoon prayer. He stopped what he was doing, pulled out his prayerbook, and began praying there on the street, "shuckling" with his usual animated devotional energy. Suddenly he found himself surrounded by a few menacing characters who turned out to be officers of the Secret Police. "They thought I was a terrorist," he recalls. He managed to avoid arrest by the skin of his teeth.

With great trepidation, the first group of students finally completed all the preparations. They got their airplane tickets, said their farewells, and set off for the United States, I-20 Visas in hand. We registered the boys into a special program of the Hadar HaTorah Foreign Students Division, and the girls were registered in Bais Rivkah. Hertzel continued to process more I-20s in Tehran, and a second group arrived in the US before Chanukah of 1978. In this group there were eleven boys, four of whom were younger than Bar Mitzvah, and also a few girls. This group was culled from the ORT school, another institution we had briefly visited in Iran.

At this point the demonstrations were becoming more frequent, and the general unrest in Iran was moving toward becoming a full-fledged revolution. Civil War had broken out, with tremendous amount of street rioting, looting, and violence. The Shah was fighting desperately for the survival of his regime. Khomeini had formed a secretive Revolutionary Council from his exile in Paris. We suddenly came to the realization that it would be necessary, sooner rather than later, to provide many more Visas for many more students.

We had to do everything possible to get the children out of Iran, ASAP. This was especially so since the Jewish leadership in Iran had indicated to us that these young men and women were now in clear and present danger. Young men were at risk of being drafted into the Iranian armies, and the young women were in other sorts of danger too terrible to consider.

What made things all the more difficult was that at that time, because of the fierce demonstrations against the Shah, with outright chaos escalating in the streets day by day, we were suddenly inundated with urgent requests to provide more I-20s. Dozens upon dozens of families were turning to the *Anjoman* Council, frantically hoping to send their sons and daughters to the United States. The *Anjoman* consulted with us in New York, and with Hertzel in Tehran. Hertzel was now working hand in hand with the local Jewish leadership. In this first intensified wave alone we received a request for 200 I-20s at one time.

It was necessary for these I-20s to be sent to Iran; the students had to actually have the I-20s with them at the time when they left the country. The American Embassy in Tehran would process them before allowing them to continue to the United States. Upon their arrival in the United States, the immigration officers at Kennedy Airport would again process their paperwork, and at that point they would be officially allowed to enter into the country as students.

Every time a group arrived at JFK during the next year and a half—usually at the old Pan Am terminal—we arranged bus transportation to Brooklyn. Members of our staff would go to JFK to meet the students, on many occasions with the help of HIAS. Several times Rabbi Hecht himself went to the airport to await them and to greet them. We were often allowed to enter the Customs and Immigration area to help the Officials process the students more quickly.

In the meantime, other sources and organizations were reaching out to us with suggestions and offers to assist. We were in constant contact with the Rebbe as to whether we should enlist the aid of these other organizations, some of whom had brought a few students in the past. The Rebbe answered that we should remain independent; his reasoning was to become increasingly clear later on, but at the time his straightforward advice sufficed. We did make several practical moves to try to make the transfers easier; HIAS (The Hebrew Immigrant Aid Society) and NYANA (the New York Association for New Americans), two long established organizations that had worked for decades with Jewish immigrants, were very helpful in many cases.

In Iran the situation went from bad to worse. In mid-January of 1979, Shah Reza Pahlavi left Iran for Egypt, ostensibly for "vacation and medical treatment." But a week later he and his family showed up in Morocco, and it wasn't long before he ran again from there, first to the Bahamas and then to Mexico. He would never return.

On the first of February, Ayatollah Khomeini returned triumphantly from his exile to Iran. News services of the time reported that up to five million people jammed the streets of Tehran to greet him. Fighting immediately broke out between rival factions in the military; martial law and curfews were imposed and ignored; guerillas and rebels swarmed into the police stations, looting them for weapons. By February eleventh the regime had collapsed, and the revolution claimed victory. It was the end of the Pahlavi dynasty, and the beginning of the Islamic Republic of Iran.

As all this was unfolding, Rabbi David Shofet called me numerous times from Tehran, early in the morning, with anguished requests to do all we could to bring as many students as we can. "The boys are being kidnapped in the streets. The girls are being attacked," he said. "We must get them out of Tehran and send them to America—to University, to Yeshiva, whatever, wherever." We stepped up our efforts, I-20 by I-20.

Though the new regime was only barely in place, the terror on the street and the universal fear of the unknown had already permeated Iranian society—and not only among the Jews. The US embassy in Tehran was soon overwhelmed with thousands of people seeking refuge, requesting travel permits and Visas of all types that would allow them to visit or emigrate to the USA.

It is difficult for us now to picture the scene in Tehran in 1979 on the streets surrounding the US Embassy. There was a curfew in effect; no one was permitted to be seen on the street between 9 pm and 6 am. But the line around the Embassy started to form much earlier in the day—until the curfew was enforced. Then what?

Disaster became the mother of ingenuity: get into your car at night, and park as close as possible to the entrance. Sleep in the car, if you can sleep at all, and at 6 am jump out and try to get to the front of the line. By 8 am the line was six to seven blocks long!

Moshe E. vividly remembers following this procedure. After several hours on line he actually got into the embassy, and moved toward the desk where an Embassy official sat. Just in front of Moshe on the line was a wealthy looking Moslem, holding a pile of official papers about four or five inches thick. Respectfully, the man approached the desk and handed document after document to the official, who patiently reviewed all the papers.

These included bank statements showing how much money the applicant had available in foreign bank accounts, ensuring that he would be able to provide for himself and his family in America. The official noted all the documentation, complimented the applicant for having provided so many detailed items, and then sent him away with all his papers. He was still missing two more pieces of paper, he told the man, and he would have to return another day to reapply.

Moshe was shaking, fearing the same reception, and praying to G-d. All he had was the I-20, a letter of support from Rabbi J.J. Hecht, and his personal ID. The official took his papers and looked him in the eye. Upon reading "Hadar Hatorah Rabbinical Seminary" on the I-20, he said, "Are you Jewish?" Moshe, terrified, shook his head in affirmation. "Be back here at 3 pm today. Your Visa will be waiting for you."

Moshe arrived in New York a few days later. He entered our system and devoted himself to his studies. A few years later he met a young woman who had come to Crown Heights around the same time. They continued their education, later married, and built a beautiful, faithful Jewish family.

A couple of times we managed to have several hundred visas processed at once and sent to Iran (more about how we accomplished this in the next chapter.) In one or two cases the names of the students had to be changed when the I-20s got to Tehran, and our people took the extraordinary step of whiting out and changing the names on the applications.

Many months later, one fine Spring day, Rabbi J.J. Hecht received a cordial visit from several gentlemen from the FBI. The agents wanted to know if we had authorized the changing of names on the I-20s. They felt that this should not have been done in that fashion (in fact it was completely illegal); perhaps this was a case of identity theft? Whether out of respect for Rabbi Hecht, or perhaps some unstated sympathy for our cause, they refrained from making it a federal case. We dodged a bullet.

In any event, starting from a few weeks after Sukkot, until Pesach of that year (5739, or 1979 on the Gregorian calendar), we had brought close to one thousand students from revolution-torn Iran to New York. Over the next year we would more than double that number . . . not, however, without considerable ongoing difficulties.

# CHAPTER IX
## Storm Clouds & Solutions
ᏟᎦᏅ

*After Khomeini came to power in Iran and replaced the old liberal regime of the Shah with his Islamic fundamentalist government, the Jews of Iran realized that they were facing a tidal wave of anti-Semitism. It wasn't always overt; but the Mullahs were highly skilled in promulgating the lie, still in vogue today, that their government was not anti-Jewish, just anti-Zionist. Whenever they wanted to crack down on Jews, all they had to say was that they had caught this or that Jew red-handed in some "criminal" action in support of Israel. That gave them the excuse to do whatever they wished.*

Despite the anxiety that had begun to grip the Jewish community in Iran, there was at first a significant effort on the part of its leaders to reach out to the Khomeini government. They were exploring whether it was possible to establish some sort of rapport, perhaps to arrange a permanent liaison to help solve problems that might arise in the future. In fact, a meeting was held between leaders of the Jewish community and Khomeini himself. Respectfully, yet passionately, the Jewish representatives expressed their concerns and fears. Khomeini assured them that the Jews would be allowed to practice their religion. Moreover, he said, the Jews would not be singled out for any persecution or anti-Semitic campaigns.

Those assurances, of course, turned out to be empty promises. Not long after that meeting, Mr. Habib Elghanian, a very prominent member of the Jewish community, was arrested on trumped up charges of spying for Israel and sentenced to death. Soon thereafter Mr. Beruchim, a member of the family who owned the Sinai Hotel where we had stayed during our initial visit to Tehran, was also arrested. Both were summarily executed by the Khomeini government.

There's a twist to the story of this tragedy, a premonition of sorts. Habib Elghanian had come to the US in spring of 1979 to visit his brother John, his son Sina, and their families and children. On the Shabbat after Pesach he attended services in our Synagogue in Forest Hills. Morad Ghadamian remembers how his father, Mr. Khalil Moradi, accompanied his dear friend Habib out of the shul after the service. Habib mentioned that he was planning to return to Iran that week. Khalil stopped him in mid-sentence and begged him, "Please—you are well known for the good work you have done all your life for Israel! You will be putting yourself in great danger! Please stay here." Habib responded that he had promised the Shah that he would do something for him, and he had to go back. The more Khalil stressed the potential threat to his life, the more Habib grew adamant.

When he arrived at the airport in Tehran, he was kidnapped by the Revolutionary Guards, and soon tortured and executed. The sadistic terrorists would not release his body for burial until the family paid 100,000 *Toman*, an Iranian unit of currency, for each bullet they used to kill him.

It was then that the Jews of Iran finally accepted the painful truth there was no use in attempting to establish any sort of liaison with this extremist, fanatical Islamist government. A large majority of the

Jewish citizens of Iran, as families and as individuals, began plotting their escape from Iran, seeking and scheming to find any way by which it would be possible to leave. For many, it would take a decade or more. Some looked toward Europe for an escape route. Others would eventually turn eastward, via the land route through Pakistan. But their concern for the children, as might be expected, came first. And even though we had begun to achieve a measure of success in bringing young people to America, there were inevitable complications every step of the way.

By the Spring of 1979 there were already a thousand young people in New York for whom we had accepted responsibility. In addition to the enormous challenges associated with housing, caring for, and seeing to the education of the students, there were other issues at hand. Some, of course, were financial concerns; but there were also less tangible matters that had to do with the expectations and mindsets of both the students arriving in the US and their parents back in Iran.

One of the stranger scenarios that developed was an unexpected resistance to authority on the part of the students. Some of those who had arrived in the US with our I-20s refused to cooperate 100% percent with the representatives of the Yeshiva and the school. Although at times there were good feelings of thanks and appreciation, sometimes instead of gratitude there was a certain antagonism and resentment. Many students did not see their move to NY as a form of salvation at all. Some of their parents, not wanting to alarm the kids (let alone alert their neighbors and the Iranian authorities, especially after the executions) had soft-pedaled the danger and the sudden evacuation. To these children, it was almost like going to camp. They imagined they'd have an easy time of it and expected first class accommodations.

It became essential, therefore, for us to provide counseling for the young men and women who were arriving under the supervision of the NCFJE and enrolling in Hadar Hatorah and Bais Rivkah. Moreover, this social/emotional aspect had to be seamlessly integrated into the educational component. We had initiated a High School level curriculum, as well as customized programs for the older boys; and the girls were similarly accommodated in special classes in Bais Rivkah. We were committed to maintaining a high standard of excellence, in Torah studies as well as in secular subjects. Not to mention the fact that we were hurriedly setting up additional programs in new schools in other locations, to create places that would serve the increasing influx.

Looking back on those days I can say without exaggeration that no "normal" person would have had the temerity to embrace such a monumental, seemingly impossible set of challenges. Miraculously, under Rabbi Hecht's direction and with the blessings of the Rebbe, we managed to set up a cohesive, effective program to care for and educate these kids, and to prepare for the hundreds more who were on the way. We were fortunate to be in a position to call upon young Iranian volunteers who had come to America earlier—young men and women who generously and empathetically reached out to our students with skillful guidance and moral support. Notable among them were several brothers from the Kesherim family, and the Chayempour family (about whom I'll presently have more to say.) Our friends Hertzel Illulian and Ben Sion Kohen, having recently arrived from Tehran, joined them as well.

Quite apart from our own funding challenges, the students too were feeling financial constraints. At that time there were legal restrictions placed on every Iranian as to the amount of money that they could take with them when leaving the country. The Iranian currency and all transactions having to do with the transfer of funds were controlled by the government. The students leaving Iran were allowed to bring with them an amount of money equivalent to approximately $3,500 dollars in American currency. Theoretically, as time went on, their families would be permitted to arrange other transfers of money to cover their expenses in the United States. But upon leaving Iran, each individual student was limited to that initial sum. They would cash in their Iranian currency at the airport in Iran and purchase American dollars there. An official document established permission for them to do this, verifying their status as students and specifying the amount.

The question of how to give proper attention and care to the students once they arrived also included making sure that the money they brought with them would be safe, and used appropriately. It was a delicate issue, and we were very concerned; our circle of helpers and advisors got together with Rabbi Hecht to address the question of what do with the students' personal funds. The younger students were especially at risk of losing their money, whether through theft or simple mismanagement. But we also felt that the older students should put their money into a bank account for safekeeping. We worked out a deal with the Bank HaPoalim branch in Queens to open an account in the name of each student, but requiring the second signature of one of the supervising Yeshiva staff. The money would always be available, but neither the student nor the responsible staff member would have the right to withdraw money by himself. Our purpose from the start was to ensure that all of this money would available to each student for his or her personal needs. There was certainly no intention of taking any of this money to be used for the Yeshiva, whether for tuition, school expenses, housing, or food; it was understood that all those costs would be met by Tzedaka, charitable donations.

Nonetheless some of the students did not understand why the money was being taken from them. Some didn't even understand exactly what a bank account was—and they had been told by their parents not to let anyone take their money. There were even a few who were so upset, they refused to pay attention to what we were telling them. In such cases it took a great deal of time and patience to clarify and explain the process. Eventually, however, all of these monies were deposited in proper bank accounts, and every individual student had access to his account. Soon thereafter they were able to begin transferring money from their parents' accounts, in the Middle-East as well as in Europe.

The Spring of 1979 also marked our first Pesach after the onset of *Escape from Iran*—a fitting, timely commemoration and celebration of our long history of liberation from exile. We hosted nearly 1,000 Iranian students that Pesach. Many had been invited to spend Pesach with local Crown Heights families;

but for most, we arranged large communal Seders. The *Sedarim* for several hundred boys took place in the "Farband" Hall on Kingston Avenue (which today houses Kolel Menachem, a Chabad educational institution). Another few hundred girls had their *Sedarim* in the Bais Rivkah Hall on Crown Street, and at the Machon Chana Dormitory Hall on President Street. We were greatly honored, and the students were thrilled, when the Lubavitcher Rebbe informed Rabbi Hecht that he would visit the Iranian *Sedarim*. The Rebbe did attend, and expressed his blessings for the children.

An especially touching detail of that first Pesach for the Persian kids was the fact that the Rebbe insisted that we prepare rice for them, according to their custom. Rice, of course, is not eaten on Passover by Ashkenazi Jews, as it falls into the category of *kitniyot*, grains that resemble forbidden wheat products. When the Rebbe entered the hall to visit the students, he also walked into the kitchen, and went so far as to lift the lids of the rice pots to have a look inside—so deeply concerned was he that the Iranian children should feel at home, and loved and respected for who they are. (In a similar vein, the Rebbe had told the students that when they wrote to him, they may write in Farsi.) He also asked us to send him some *maror*, the bitter herbs from the

Persian Seder, to taste a bit of their bitter experience himself.

Meanwhile, while all this was going on, we had to focus on finding first-rate faculty members and administrative staff for our schools. It was not a simple matter by any means. The students generally had good backgrounds in math and science; we wanted to make sure our school would provide them with a secular education that was precisely designed to meet them on their level, so they would feel that they were gaining and growing in their knowledge.

But the first order of business was to advertise for and hire teachers of ESL, English as a Second Language. At that time in New York City there was a great deal of emphasis on ESL programs in high schools around the city, as well as in universities, due to the strong presence of various immigrant groups. With such a high level of expertise on the market, we were able to hire a sufficient number of well-trained professionals in ESL. To establish our high school programs as capable of administering Regents Exams and issuing NY State Regents diplomas, we arranged with one of the Yeshiva high schools to work under their umbrella, as a chartered high school in New York State.

Finding the right educators proved to be a double-edged challenge. On the one hand we needed math and social studies teachers who were able to teach children who had already achieved a relatively advanced level of knowledge. But when it came to finding rabbinical teachers for students who lacked a solid background in *Limudei Kodesh* (Torah studies), the opposite was true; most classes had to be on a beginners' level. The language gap was also an issue. Some kids spoke a little bit of Hebrew, some a little English . . . but it soon became clear that we needed to find teachers who could speak to the children in their language. We did find several individuals in the community who could speak Farsi, and they were able to get the ball rolling for the first few months. Eventually we succeeded in bringing Rabbi Eliyahu Ben Chaim from Tehran, a *Rebbe* par excellence in the area of teaching *Limudei Kodesh*, in Farsi, to the Iranian children and Avi Nissanian and Avi Nissanian, two Farsi speaking cousins who had arrived from Israel. As the weeks went by, their knowledge of English and Hebrew advanced to the point that we were able to hire American and Israeli teachers to provide a full range of excellent *Limudei Kodesh* classes.

Then there was the question of where to situate all this amazing activity. At first, for the boys, we held classes in the NCFJE headquarters at 824 Eastern Parkway, which also housed Hadar HaTorah. After a few weeks we ran out of room. Through the good graces of the venerable *Hassid* Rabbi Micheol

Teitelbaum of Yeshiva Oholei Torah, we were able to use a building in East Flatbush, Brooklyn, just a ten-minute drive from Eastern Parkway. There were several very nice classrooms in a Shul on East 53rd street where he had been a *Chazzan Sheini* and *Shammas* for many years, and where he still had proprietorship. As it worked out, that building also had a dining room and kitchen, so we were able to provide breakfast and lunch in the same building where they attended class. That became the first annex to our Yeshiva.

Following that there were other places in Crown Heights where we found workable classrooms. That sufficed for a short while, but the kids kept coming. The next place we managed to occupy was a facility made available by our friend Mr. Irwin Cohen and his group, on Mott Avenue in Far Rockaway. We were able to arrange for a dormitory as well as classroom facilities in that building. Although it entailed busing the students back and forth from Crown Heights to Far Rockaway, nevertheless it served its purpose.

By May of 1979, and then again with the new school year (and many more new students) in the Fall, we actually had a fully functioning high school. It was somewhat geographically dispersed, but we were proud (and amazed!) to be delivering a full, optimum-quality course of both secular studies and

*Limudei Kodesh*. By this point most of the kids spoke English to the point where we were able to make English the main language of instruction.

Once the school was established, we had to create an administration. Rabbi Yossi Raichik, of blessed memory, was appointed Principal of the Yeshiva. He assumed responsibility for organizing the curriculum, arranging for the teachers, composing syllabi for the various classes, facilitating all the in-service teacher training and student counseling involved in the schooling of the students, and ensuring that they were given everything they required for a proper education.

By September of 1979 we had brought somewhere between 1,200–1,300 Iranian students to the United States. Many of these students had made contact with relatives, friends, or siblings who had come to America earlier; little by little, some began to request to be transferred to other Yeshivot. In many cases this was tricky, as it also became necessary to reissue their I-20s to indicate a new educational institution. Notwithstanding this difficulty we began the process of transferring students to other schools. Eventually we expedited successful transfers to several dozen Yeshivot of their own choice, all over the United States, where they continued their high school or college education.

During the last months of 1979 and extending into the summer of 1980, several hundred new students arrived. This kept up until the end of 1980, with more arriving all the time. By this time we were regularly transferring a significant number of students out to other schools and other places. So at that time we were only accommodating approximately 400 students in our boys' schools, and about 200 attending various classes in the women's schools in Crown Heights. By June of 1981, the majority of the children had either graduated or requested transfers to other areas, other schools, other cities, and other Yeshivot. By September of 1981 there was only a small number continuing on in the programs we had set up. At that point many of the students had qualified for transfers into the existing Yeshivot in Crown Heights, primarily to either the Lubavitcher Yeshiva High School, or Oholei Torah High School, or into the main Yeshiva Gedolah which was centered at 770 Eastern Parkway.

For two full years we had run a full-scale, chartered, Regents-level High School with both a Jewish studies and a Secular studies curriculum. We met the challenge, we organized the classes, we employed the teachers, and we provided the venues and the locations of the schools. Years later, reflecting on all the efforts and dedication put forward by the members of our team, we can proudly say that hundreds of Iranian children, who, had they stayed in Iran would not have received a full-fledged Jewish education, were given the finest Jewish education one could ask for in the United States. Moreover, as a result of the educational aspects of the operation, the Iranian Jewish community in America at the present time comprises hundreds if not thousands of families who are knowledgeable in Torah and who are passionate in their observance of Torah and Mitzvahs. Having taken upon themselves to live their Jewish lives according to the true tradition of *Yahadut Paras*, the Jews of Persia have brought honor and glory back to their history as Iranian Jews, 2,500 years after the destruction of the Beit HaMikdash.

# CHAPTER X
## Heroism at Home & Abroad
ᏏᏬ

*In January of 1979 we received a desperate call: "Deliver 200 I-20s to London tomorrow, or 200 students will be stranded here." We had no computers, no laser printers; even electric typewriters were a luxury in those days. It was an impossible task.*

*Our young Persian Jewish volunteer Moshe Chayempour was there in the office, seated next to me at the conference table. He rose to his feet and announced with unshakeable certainty, "I'll take care of it, **ya'allah**!" He grabbed a stack of I-20 forms and darted out the door.*

***Ya'allah** was an Arabic expression Moshe used often; he meant, "This is for the sake of Heaven!"—and he insisted it never fails. At*

*eight the next morning he strode in with 200*
*completed I-20s. They were on the next plane*
*to London, and that night 200 more students*
*made their way to us. It would be years before*
*Moshe revealed to us the secret of how he got*
*it done.*

Back in Iran, while we were struggling night
and day in New York to welcome the 1,000-
plus children and set up the schools, Rabbi David
Shofet was experiencing a different sort of difficulty.
Beyond assembling the lists of prospective students,
a big part of his participation in the project was
explaining to the parents the complexities and the
challenges of the operation. It wasn't easy to leave
Iran. So in the Spring of 1979 we composed a formal
letter to Rabbi Shofet to assist him in that task, clar-
ifying the scope of our activities, the conditions of
the hospitality and programs we offered, and at least
some of the expenses incurred.

We described all the various educational institutions involved—high school and college level, boys
and girls, classroom buildings and dorms, tutoring
and counseling, right down to an itemized report
on the daily schedules of classes, subjects taught,
mealtimes, sports, and recreation. We gave detailed
accounts of our attention to their cultural adjust-

ment, medical care, and individualized language skills; feeding, clothing, and housing the kids; bowling, skiing, and swimming; excursions in the big city to museums, planetariums, the Statue of Liberty and Madison Square Garden . . .

Up until the point when the sheer numbers of students became overwhelming, we hadn't asked the Iranian parents for any contributions to tuition and housing costs. In our letter to Rabbi Shofet we reiterated our policy of having the children deposit their personal money in a savings account, with a savings book for withdrawals and deposits, and informed him as to how, for their own protection, we were holding their passports for safekeeping. There had been some confusion regarding the opening of the bank accounts, as virtually every one of the students had been told by their parents not to give their own money up; so we took great pains to clarify our policy with total transparency.

Once the large numbers of students had intensified our financial burden to the breaking point, we asked Rabbi Shofet to inform the parents that the official fee for the entire program had been set at $6,000 per year, per student. Nonetheless we also stipulated that we would provide scholarships for those who for whatever reason were unable to pay. Rabbi Shofet would be in charge of assessing a family's need for financial aid and advise us as to how much those families could pay—just as he had supervised the prioritization of which students would receive their visas first. With all that, it was made clear that Rabbi Hecht would continue to be the responsible party for the overall cost of the entire operation. In actuality very little money was raised through tuition. A majority of the families were sticking to their position that the rich American community should be able to cover the expenses of the programs that were taking care of their children.

We also urged Rabbi Shofet to emphasize that although we were volunteering to help the students in their quest for safety, we were neither encouraging nor coercing them to leave. This was important for at least two reasons. On the one hand we didn't want to fan the flames of panic on the war-torn, oppressive streets of Tehran, by giving the impression that we were "saving" the Jewish kids from a terrible fate that everyone was facing, not just the Jews. And our experience with the first waves of students in New York had shown us how crucial it was that the children understand how their well-being rested in the hands of the Director of the program. Their attitude could either make or break their own success.

As our early efforts grew into a major operation of daunting proportion, Rabbi Hecht gathered together a group of people to work with him. Hertzel Illulian and I were of course already up to our elbows in the project, and remained that way (my family will attest to the fact that I wasn't home much during those intense two years). Yossi Raichik, who had returned to America from Israel and Iran around that first Rosh Hashanah, was another principal player. So were Aryeh Sufrin, Mendel Kotlarsky, and Shabsi Chaiton, who worked tirelessly to ensure the daily welfare and comfort of the students. Several rabbinical students studying in 770 also volunteered and worked very closely with us. Later on Aryeh Sufrin woke early every morning to drive the students by bus to classes in other neighborhoods. When Ben Sion Kohen, our faithful driver from Tehran, arrived in the United States, we drafted him to be on the staff. Then suddenly, out of nowhere, Moshe Chayempour appeared.

Moshe Chayempour had emigrated to America a number of years earlier and attended the New Jersey Institute of Technology, earning a Master's degree in fluid mechanics and engineering. Coming from a very religious family, he had a strong traditional background, yet was by nature somewhat skeptical. An Iranian friend who was at that time learning in Yeshiva invited him to a *Pegisha*, a weekend "Encounter with Chabad" geared mostly toward college students. Soon thereafter he began taking courses at the Rabbinical College of America in Morristown, NJ, while also teaching in university. Before long his true character as a person of deep faith and *yirat Shamayim* (devotion to the demands of spiritual life) had blossomed; he showed up one day in our offices at 824 Eastern Parkway and volunteered to help.

Moshe became one of the most powerful driving forces in the entire movement to bring Iranian students to America. He worked tirelessly, 24/7, for two full years, many times sleeping on a couch in our office. He was involved with the students once they came, in the dormitories and in the schools, working with them on a personal basis as a mentor and counselor. He became our go-to person who somehow was able to get things done that no one else could accomplish—sometimes leveraging his technical knowledge and contacts in academia, sometimes by simple force of will, and sometimes because miracles seemed to follow him around. The 200 I-20s he produced overnight, we eventually learned, had been typed up in a state-of-the-art multiple-typewriter chain linked to a master typewriter, owned by an Israel friend of his in Manhattan. Once when he and Hertzel and I were returning from a trip upstate to oversee our summer camp for the Persian kids, he managed (it seemed) to hypnotize a state trooper

who had pulled us over for speeding. When he and
Yossi Raichik once had to fly to London to deliver
I-20s, they were busy in the office preparing paperwork until 7:10 P.M., then left to catch a 7:50 flight at
JFK. Impossible. But somehow the pilot of the plane
knew he had to delay the flight and open the gate for
them when they arrived.

Not long after we started bringing Iranian students to the US, before the American Embassy in
Tehran was overrun by Islamist radicals, we began to
sense a slowdown at the Embassy in putting through
our I-20 applications. Soon thereafter the US State
Department sent a memo to Rabbi Abraham Shemtov,
Chabad's principal liaison to government officials in
Washington. The memo gave us formal notice that
due to the deteriorating political situation in Iran,
the staff in the US Embassy had been cut, and non-
essential workers were sent home. Because it would
take too long, Tehran would no longer be able to effectively process the many applications. Rabbi Hecht
called us all together for a meeting to come up with
alternative places through which we could route the
students and send the I-20s. Hertzel Illulian, having
been born and raised in Italy, had many connections
there; he suggested sending the students from Tehran to Rome, where they could be processed and
then sent on to New York. Our contacts at the Joint

Distribution Committee and HIAS confirmed the likelihood that the Persian students could easily get visitor's visas to Italy, and that from Rome we could arrange for student visas and bring them to the US from there. At the same meeting Moshe Chayempour suggested that London would also serve as an additional venue. Rabbi Shemtov forwarded our ideas to Washington, and the State Department agreed that we should go ahead with the plan.

Hertzel, with his great command of the language, spent that summer in Italy setting up the procedures and working with the students. There were occasional delays, but most were ironed out rather smoothly with assistance of HIAS, as well as the senior Chabad emissary in Italy, Rabbi Moshe Lazar, who had also established strong connections with the Persian Jewish community in Milan.

That August Moshe Chayempour travelled to London to facilitate similar operations there. In England, however, the delays were more problematic; complications in the processing of paperwork sometimes necessitated finding places for many of the Iranian students for several weeks or more. In fact Moshe had to return to London after that summer to galvanize the team that would handle such difficulties. He and Yossi Raichik, plus Meir Rhodes, another American activist who had become involved, worked together with the local Chabad leadership—Rabbis Vogel, Jaffe, Sufrin, and Lew—to house and feed the now steady influx of students while their visas were in limbo. Some were placed in private homes. Carmel College, a Jewish boarding school not far from London that served a substantial number of international students also accommodated the Persian students, not just with food and lodging but attending classes as well. Some of the younger students were accepted into the Jewish summer camps while waiting for their papers to come through.

While these difficulties required enormous effort, far more serious obstacles arose after the violent attack on the US Embassy in Tehran in November of 1979. Five hundred radical Islamist students stormed the heavily-defended building and captured sixty-six American hostages—a world-shattering event that would take 444 days to resolve (though the Islamic revolution still reverberates throughout the world today). A sign of those times: El Al announced that any Jew who could was welcome to board the last planes flying out of Tehran to Israel, gratis, before the Airline shut down its operation in Iran. And another strange anecdote sheds light on the extent to which Persian Jewry had become so profoundly assimilated, many barely recognized the danger they were in. When US President Carter's attempt to send commandos to rescue the hostages failed tragically, some of the Iranian students actually celebrated Khomeini's victory.

A few weeks after the Embassy takeover, the US State Department came up with yet another wrench in the works. Fearing that our 1-20 papers and student visas would enable the covert infiltration of Islamist terrorists into America, they ruled in early 1980 that no more I-20s would be processed for our students. The transit points we had established in Italy and England were no longer functional; this happened just as a group of sixty Iranian students arrived in London. (This particular cohort of students was not from Tehran, but from Isfahan, one of the cities we had been unable to visit during our original trip due to the early unrest that was just beginning at that time.) Now trapped in London, these students needed to be housed for what was then an unpredictable period of time. Moshe Chayempour once again rolled up his sleeves and went to work.

Back in the States, Rabbi Hecht and Rabbi Shemtov had exerted rigorous effort over several months in reaching out to the State Department to right this wrong. They worked their way up the bureaucratic channels and finally reached to the level of Stuart Eizenstat, a special counsel to President Carter and liaison between the White House and the Jewish community. Rabbi Hecht made a powerful case on behalf of our students: all of them were known members of the Jewish community, had been carefully vetted every step of the way, had been oppressed themselves by the Iranian regime, were unquestionably loyal to American values, and were seeking freedom in the West. Finally, in August of 1980, the ban was lifted, the I-20s were issued, and amidst great joy and jubilation the students boarded their flight to the United States.

Little did they know that yet another obstruction would arise. Upon landing at JFK Airport and arriving in the Customs and Immigration area, there was suddenly great tumult as they were informed that the consular officers at JFK had been told not to admit any Iranians with I-20s. Evidently the approval that had been delivered to London had not yet been conveyed to the officials in the US; they were told they would have to board a plane and return to London. Moshe Chayempour, who had arrived in New York on a previous flight, was beside himself. He called NCFJE immediately and a few minutes later Rabbi Hecht appeared at the airport.

One of the Iranian students who was on that flight vividly recalls seeing Rabbi Hecht, pacing rapidly among the Immigration officers, gesticulating vociferously in his characteristic flamboyant manner, demanding satisfaction but getting none. Finally he put through a call to Washington. It's not clear by all accounts with whom he spoke—it may have been Eizenstat, or Rabbi Shemtov, or the White House, or all three—but within an hour or two the Airport officials were informed that clearance had been granted. All the Iranian students who were on that plane with I-20s issued under the auspices of Hadar HaTorah Yeshiva and signed by Rabbi Hecht were to be given their visas and allowed into the United States. They were then driven directly from JFK to the newly acquired property in Far Rockaway which we had redesigned as a dormitory and school.

## The Game Change Challenge

By the time of the overthrow of the Embassy in Tehran, 1,500 students had been brought to the US. Every time a new group arrived from Iran they were like refugees, having left their homeland and experienced great emotional stress. Our staff spared no effort to place and keep the new arrivals in a serene and comfortable environment. Many local residents in Crown Heights sacrificed their own comfort to make room for them in their homes. Setting them up in our various dormitories, always seeking new spaces that could be adapted for them, we were thrilled to be able to provide them with their first breath of air in America, and the first meals they received.

At the beginning of the process the Hadar HaTorah students in their dorm rooms gladly doubled and tripled up to accommodate them. Apartments were temporarily rented for the overflow, until we were fortunate enough to gain access to a building several blocks away at 570 Eastern Parkway. Again, it was Moshe Chayempour who stepped up to make the top floors of that building into dorm rooms, and the bottom floors into classrooms, all the while acting as a compassionate role model for the boys. Bais Rivkah also really went out of its way with their facilities in providing space for the girls from the Iranian community; and we managed to eke out some extra space in the dorm of our women's seminary for beginners, Machon Chana, a twenty-five-room former mansion on President Street. Under the auspices of Hadar HaTorah we gradually were able to move students into several other buildings, arranging them into dormitories, kitchens, dining rooms, and classrooms.

It was always touch and go. There was one disturbing incident which took place in an eight-family building on the corner of Eastern Parkway and Albany Avenue, owned by a resident of Crown Heights who graciously allowed us to use it rent free. Rabbi Hecht's twin sons Shimon and Levi, my younger brothers, were volunteering at the time, and took charge of the renovations, speedily installing beds and furniture. We decided to assign those rooms to a group of the older Iranian girls. This was the winter of 1980 and it was freezing cold, so the boiler was activated to heat the building as the girls were moving in. But the building had not been used in several years, and apparently the boiler flue was not functioning properly. Suddenly the place was filled with smoke and the stench of burning oil. Panic ensued, as several dozen young Persian students were forced to evacuate the building and stood shivering out on the street. But not for long. Rabbi Hecht directed his son Levi to find the nearest hotel that could accommodate all the girls. In a matter of minutes a caravan of vehicles—including Rabbi Hecht's car—swept them away and up toward La Guardia Airport, where we had booked them into comfortable rooms at the Hilton Hotel for a few nights until the furnace could be repaired.

Then came a huge game changer. A group of doctors who owned the once-thriving, now defunct Lefferts General Hospital building, recognizing the needs of the Iranian children, came to Rabbi Hecht and offered to sell him the building for a very low price.

The doctors came to meet with Rabbi Hecht in his office on Eastern Parkway. They presented a very rosy picture of the building's potential and offered a bargain price. An agreement was reached, papers and checks were signed, and Rabbi Hecht undertook one of the greatest projects of his life, to take over that enormous building and render it usable for many hundreds of Iranian boys who had been saved and brought to America.

You cannot imagine the absolute state of shock and the terrible letdown Rabbi Hecht experienced when he actually visited the hospital and found—contrary to the way it had been represented—that the building had been completely gutted! All of the pipes had been ripped out of the walls, all the electric fixtures had been torn from the ceilings, doors were missing from the doorways, and windows had been smashed. The hospital building looked like it had been hit by a tsunami.

With this great challenge staring him in the face, Rabbi Hecht heroically lifted himself out of despondency and immediately rolled up his sleeves. We gathered together a group of donors and hired contractors to start to make the building livable. The problem was that space was needed immediately, and no matter how diligently the contractors worked it would still take a lot of time to get the pipes, electric lines, windows, and doors replaced.

Mr. Charlie Kupferman had known Rabbi Hecht since his childhood. In fact, while he was still a young boy in public school he had attended Release Time Classes, an innovative Jewish educational program operating from Rabbi Hecht's office and conducted by young volunteer teachers. Now working in his newly established Brooklyn real estate business, Charlie became aware of the overwhelming difficulties facing the Iranian students project and offered his expert advice and recommendations. With Charlie at his side, and despite the escalating financial problems that jeopardized his ability to pay the contractors, Rabbi Hecht managed to push through the staggering amount of work needed at Lefferts General Hospital. Over the next few weeks, rooms became available one by one, and were readied to serve as dormitory facilities for the Iranian boys.

At about the same time Rabbi Hecht turned his attention to the building next door, at 828 Eastern Parkway. A four-story walk up comprised of eight apartments, it had originally been purchased as an extension of the Hadar HaTorah Yeshiva, some time before the Iranian students began to arrive. However by the time all the tenants had moved out and some minor renovations had begun, the priorities had shifted. Rabbi Hecht asked Charlie Kupferman to take a look at the building and advise him as to how to change eight apartments into a dormitory, classrooms, and offices.

"Not easy," said Charlie, as he surveyed the rotted plumbing and old galvanized water pipes peeking through the broken walls. It needed new floors for the bathrooms, new copper pipes for the hot and cold water, and a major realignment of walls and halls. Charlie recommended plumbing contractors, carpenters, electricians, and tile workers. The vision was to create the maximum possible number of dorm rooms on the third and fourth floors, with the first floor housing the office of school. Although it was not foreseen at the time, the second floor would eventually become the Persian Jewish Center of Brooklyn. And so the work began.

While 828 was undergoing its conversion, the owners of a few other buildings in the neighborhood volunteered to provide temporary space for classes and dormitories. And about fifteen minutes away, on East 53rd Street, two more centers were drafted into service for the Persian kids. The Jewish community of East Flatbush had been greatly downsized in recent years, so the daily use of these local shuls was minimized. One was Rabbi Hecht's Shul, Yeshiva Rabbi Meir Simcha HaKohen, whose large Beis

Medrash auditorium provided ample space for the newly arrived groups. It became the base of incoming registration. There the students were given their first meal while all the paper work was being handled. The second shul was Bnei Avraham, under the stewardship of Rav Michoel Teitelbaum, where we set up classrooms, a kitchen, and a dining room.

Just looking at the surface reality of this seemingly overwhelming stream of refugees, one could be forgiven for thinking that Crown Heights was under siege. But what was really happening was that a community was being reborn.

At a glance, it may have seemed that the Lubavitcher Rebbe was advising us and guiding the operation in two conflicting ways. On the one hand he felt very strongly that for the sake of the Iranian children's education, they must be welcomed and remain for as long as possible in Crown Heights. With us, they would not only receive schooling of the highest caliber, they would be able to stay faithful to their own Persian and Sefaradi customs and traditions, in a warm and accepting community. And yet when Rabbi Hecht asked the Rebbe whether the parents of the children should be encouraged to come to America, or to go to Israel, he clearly expressed his point of view that we should advise the adults to go to Israel. In Israel they would find themselves in a society where kosher food is everywhere, where they would be able and inspired to observe Shabbat, and where they would be steeped in a rich and vibrant Jewish environment. Whereas in America, they would more likely have been subject to the influence of a Jewish milieu that is largely assimilated and out of touch with tradition. In Iran, many had drifted toward assimilation; in America they would be all the more susceptible to further assimilation.

This was the brilliance of the Rebbe's vision: the children's education in America, combined with their parents' renewed sense of their Jewishness in Israel, would before long restore and reinvigorate the quality of Iranian Jewish life. Having been rescued from the ravages of revolution, the inherent strength of their commitment to family and cultural continuity would ensure that they'd soon be reunited, and thrive.

# CHAPTER XI
## Diaspora Rising
ભ્જ

*One of the youngest children among the thousands we brought from Iran during the years of* Escape from Iran *was a ten-year-old girl named Mersedeh Eshagian. She had been orphaned from her father the year before we met her, and her widowed mother believed that her best (or perhaps only) opportunity for a good life would be to come to America and escape a frightful, uncertain future in Iran. Her story is a long odyssey of heartbreak and hope, aloneness and loving care. Though her Jewish family of origin was hardly observant, today she is a religious woman living a rich, Torah-true life. When you ask her how her mother allowed a child of such tender age to*

*travel to a foreign country of unfamiliar culture
and language, she replies that her mother had
heard the Rabbi from New York speaking in
the synagogue, and she knew she could put her
trust in him.*

The education of the several thousand Iranian students we brought to America was a significant factor in the course of enabling tens of thousands of Persian Jewish families to eventually leave Iran. With their children becoming more and more settled and increasingly familiar with the customs, the language, the community structure, and other aspects of life in the United States, their parents felt they had a foothold here. Many of them had been able to transfer their assets to America, either via their children who were here as students, or through other avenues. It was all part of a large, complex, Divinely conceived plan to establish a new Persian Jewish community in the American hemisphere that would prove to be both materially and spiritually enriched, as never before.

It's also interesting to consider why the Iranian Jewish exodus to America went so much more smoothly than efforts to rescue Jewish citizens from other Middle Eastern Muslim countries. The Jews of Yemen, Morocco, Egypt, Algeria, Libya, and Iraq experienced great difficulty in obtaining visas, for example, to the US, whereas the State Department had a far more open attitude toward Iranian immigration. In part this may have been due to the relative wealth of the Iranian Jewish community, as distinct from the impoverished citizenry of these other Islamic strongholds. Culture may also have been a factor, inasmuch as Iranian Jewry were in general better educated and more cosmopolitan. But one cannot underestimate the profound impact of Rabbi Hecht's influence, as he was in such frequent contact and dialogue with US government officials on behalf of our rescue efforts. He presented compelling portrayals of the dangers these sincere and capable students faced in the war-torn revolutionary milieu of Iran; and his arguments reached all the way up to the White House, convincing the 'powers that be' to confer upon them refugee status. In an extraordinary letter to Rabbi Hecht (reproduced in the Appendix), US Congressman Stephen Solarz wrote, "Knowing of your deep concern for the thousands of Iranians who have taken refuge in our country, I wanted you to know that I learned recently that the State Department has begun to process the 9,000 asylum applications filed by Iranians . . . If any problems arise in the treatment of these applications, which are confidential, I would appreciate your contacting me immediately."

There were, of course, bumps along the way. At times, rather than collaboration and mutual appreciation, there was some antagonism, misunderstanding, or bad feelings between the administration and some of the students, or among various leadership factions in America. Over time, most of these problems ironed themselves out. Rabbi Hecht was admired as a leader truly dedicated to the well-being of the refugees, as people came to recognize the great self-sacrifice he had to have in order to get and keep the program running. Rebbetzin Hecht too became a mentor and guide to many of the young women, especially through Camp Emunah and other programs for girls. Families in Crown Heights volunteered in droves to accept girls into their homes, whether to move in, or for meals on Shabbos and Yom Tov. The broad feeling of cooperation and responsibility was deepened by the realization that the Rebbe was so strongly in the favor of super-human efforts of the community on behalf of these immigrants. Whenever possible, people went out of their way to try to help.

We also had tremendous support from various segments of the New York Persian community, especially during the early months of the Foreign Students Division we established in our Brooklyn Yeshiva. By 1978 there was already a sizable group of

Persian expatriates living in the United States. A few of the families had been here for many years; others had arrived in the 1970s, some from Tehran, Shiraz, or Isfahan, and still others from Hamedan, which had been the ancient Persian capital of Shushan Habirah. This mixture of Iranian Jews in the United States provided the backdrop against which the exodus began. In fact, at the Sephardic Congregation in Queens where I served as Rabbi, there were a number of Persian families who had been in Queens and Long Island since the 1960s. Among them were businessmen, active in importing Persian rugs, in clothing manufacturing, in real estate, in jewelry and diamonds. There were also builders and engineers, and many professionals—especially in the field of medicine.

During the years of the Shah's reign there had been a certain tolerance, even benevolence, toward Jews. Jewish families who wanted their children to be doctors often sent their sons to Paris, as there had been a good relationship between France and Iran dating back to the 1950s. Some of them returned to Iran after receiving their degrees, to serve as doctors in Tehran and other cities. It has been estimated that in 1978, 10% of the doctors in Tehran were Jewish. Others, however, either remained in France or emigrated to the United States, where they would serve as doctors after passing the US exams. Several of them settled in the Forest Hills area, became members of our Congregation, and stepped up with great generosity to offer their time and expertise to the young Iranian students we were bringing to America. One of the most prominent Persian doctors from Queens who volunteered to care for students without pay was Dr. Mozzafar Bakhchi, a pediatrician, who established a well-equipped infirmary in our NCFJE building at 824 Eastern Parkway. One morning per week, every week, he would hold office hours in his little infirmary, examining and treating anyone with medical problems, or even who simply did not feel well. Dr. Said Dounel, an OB-GYN, also volunteered his time and took special care of the young women in the program. He too would come to Brooklyn on a regular basis to provide medical care free of charge.

Another member of the Sephardic Congregation in Queens, one of the original people with whom we had consulted about our plans, was Mr. Aziz Halimi, a highly respected *gabbai* in our Congregation and a successful entrepreneur. When the students started to arrive, he came to Brooklyn often to speak with them, encouraging them to disregard the small difficulties and envision the great opportunities that lay ahead. He would share his own experiences as a young man new to America who overcame many obstacles during his years in University to achieve success in the United States. And as I have mentioned previously, Mr. Azaria Levy, senior member of the esteemed Levy family of Kew Gardens, was also among the key players among the Persian Jewish locals, supporting and reinforcing our programs for the refugees. Representing the Mashhadi community, he was also held in high regard in the community at large.

As was the aforementioned Mr. Khalil Moradi, who together with Azariah Levy contributed greatly to our initial forays into Iran. Mr. Moradi had visited in the US from his Iranian home in the city of Hamedan in the early 1960s. He also visited Baltimore, where, because he so greatly valued Torah education, he enrolled his sons in the famed Ner Yisrael Yeshivah. Eventually he moved to New York, where he became a very successful "broker," as he referred to himself—an importer and exporter of a wide variety of quality goods between Iran, other Middle Eastern and Far Eastern countries, and the United States. As a man of unshakeable faith and commitment to Jewish tradition and community, he took a strong interest in our project and in our students, developing warm and productive relationships and generously supporting our programs across the board. Not only did he often visit with us and the newcomers to Crown Heights himself, he also encouraged his own sons to take an interest in the needs and the well-being of the students.

Mr. Moradi's piety was deeply respected, especially for his predisposition toward *mattan b'seter*, giving charity anonymously, inasmuch as *tzedakah*, charitable giving, is so highly regarded among the members of our synagogue. His integrity served as a shining example and a high standard of accomplishment, widely emulated by members of our community in Queens. Although he had never studied in an established Yeshiva—his formal education was clearly on the level of the training he had received in his youth, in Hamedan—he always aspired to deepen his study of Torah and improve his level of observance.

To his dying day, Khalil Moradi attended daily services, making special arrangements for his son to bring him to the synagogue for the morning prayers. I personally took great inspiration during the High Holidays, when he insisted on having his seat placed near the *Bima*, close to the *Heichal* where the Holy Ark resides.

Due to his solid connections with Ner Yisrael in Baltimore, Mr. Moradi put a lot of effort into establishing a liaison between our work and the administration there. Ner Yisrael had a long-standing relationship

with the Jewish community in the Iranian city of Shiraz. A small Yeshiva there, led by Rabbi Baal Haness,
used to send a few top students to study in America at
Ner Yisrael from time to time. In fact several Iranian
graduates had moved from Baltimore to Los Angeles,
where they were able to serve as true Torah leaders for
Iranian emigres who had settled there.

At a certain point in the process of our operation,
the national orthodox Jewish advocacy organization
Agudath Yisrael became interested in pursuing rescue efforts of their own. They approached Ner Yisrael
and other schools, asking them to provide I-20s for
the students to whom they were reaching out. Agudath Yisrael also had contacts in the Iranian Jewish
community in Queens. When Mr. Moradi became
aware of the shared purpose of the two programs,
he urged Ner Yisrael to coordinate with Rabbi Hecht
in New York, and was bitterly disappointed when
the Principal of Ner Yisrael declined to collaborate
with us, feeling that the two organizations—Aguda
and Chabad—could not or would not effectively work
together. Because of his love for the Jewish people
and his strong belief in our essential unity despite
our differences, he was very hurt by what he considered a missed opportunity.

As it turned out, there were some students
accepted into several other schools around the coun-

try through these efforts. Later on, after thousands had been brought to America through the system we had established, we worked very hard to facilitate the transfer of many Iranian students to these various other institutions, especially in areas where they had relatives or friends.

The diaspora of Persian Jews was widespread, and on the move; interestingly, the particular groups emerging from their various cities and communities of origin tended to retain their own character and customs. The Mashhadi community, for example, having been at one point largely relocated from Mashhad to Tehran, then dispersed to many other areas around the globe—to Milan, Italy, where Rabbi Moshe Lazar served as the Rabbi of the Persian con-

In their desire to accommodate the arriving students, there were some misguided zealots who approached the students at the airport and advised them not to go with "the Chabad group." Sadly, some students followed this imprudent advice and ended up in inappropriate schools. It was with great difficulty that we managed to straighten out the official papers.

gregation; to London, England, and other cities in Europe; and also to the United States, including New York City and Los Angeles—yet largely remained in cohesive groups that identified proudly as Mashhadi.

The Jewish community in the Iranian city of Isfahan was somewhat less assimilated than those in other cities, with a higher level of Jewish observance and tradition. To a significant extent this can be attributed to the fact that the local Etehad school there had instituted a curriculum offering considerably more robust Judaic content than the other branches of the Alliance network. Each day there were classes in Jewish history, in Talmud, and *Tanach* (Biblical studies.) The spiritual leaders in Isfahan, Rabbi Shimon Yadegeran and Rabbi Yitzchak Rabbani, were well loved and admired in the community. They gave their blessing in May of 1980 to a group of sixty students to join our program in New York. This was the group mentioned earlier, whose journey had been impeded by the sudden cessation of visas by the US State Department, who had gotten stuck in London, and then were nearly deported immediately upon arrival in New York.

The full scope and success of an operation of this magnitude, with its thousands of beneficiaries, can perhaps be best appreciated by examining the detailed experience of a few individuals. One of the students in this group from Isfahan was a seventeen-year-old boy from a religious family, an excellent student from the Etehad School named Shlomo Mahgerefteh. Forced to remain in England, he was fortunate at first to be welcomed by a kind and hospitable British Jewish family for six weeks, then transferred to an Iranian family in London, where he was treated with great respect and care. It wasn't until August of that year that Rabbi Hecht succeeded in prevailing upon the State Department to lift the decree; after much drama the group was admitted. Shlomo was among the students who had a wonderful month at the end of that summer in our Day Camp facility in Far Rockaway, and then were transferred to the Yeshiva in Crown Heights. By that time we had brought over nearly two thousand students, expanded our boarding facilities, and continued to develop our curricula in both Torah studies and English subjects. Until today Shlomo remembers with fondness and great appreciation for his two devoted Jewish studies teachers in that school year of 1980–81, Rabbi Shapiro and Rabbi Levitin. He continued on to the Lubavitch Yeshiva on Ocean Parkway and then was among the 150 students we placed in Touro College in Manhattan. He returned to live in Crown Heights after graduation, married, went into business, lives today in Kew Gardens, Queens, and retains close ties with the Crown Heights community where he had spent so many years. Shlomo's younger brother David Margerefteh was among many others who followed similar paths; having arrived from Iran with a cohort of 170 students, David eventually graduated from NYU Podiatry school and now serves as a respected Doctor in Queens.

Mersedeh Eshagian's story is another illustrative tale of the powerful effect our galvanized community had on the lives of so many refugees. Having been among the girls we had to whisk away from the smoky furnace at the dorm facility (see Chapter X), before long she was welcomed into the home of the wonderful Goldman family in Crown Heights. Mrs. Esther Goldman had arranged an apartment in her home for a number of girls, served lovingly as a surrogate mother, and even helped them with their homework at night. Then after an exhilarating summer vacation at Camp Emunah under the care of Rebbetzin Hecht, and a brief stint as a mother's helper for a Lubavitcher family, Mersedeh was "adopted" by the Shaya Boymelgreen family, who cared for her as though she were one of their own children. For a time they employed her in their real estate business; and when she married they made all the arrangements for her wedding. As a young girl Mersedeh was chosen by Rabbi Hecht to address the gathering at one the NFCJE annual dinners at the Sheraton Hotel, where she spoke poignantly to the assembled guests, sharing the many harrowing details of her journey, pouring out her heart, telling of her fears and gratitude and hopes for the future.

One of the most well-known core teachings of Chassidic philosophy reveals the true value that is concealed within adversity: the light that emerges out of darkness is far brighter—perhaps infinitely greater—than light that has been steadily present in "normal" circumstances. Mersedeh represents one small case in point: even after being rescued from Iran and being blessed with the finest education and loving care, tragedy struck. She lost her beloved husband to an illness that took his life. And it didn't end there; she had to rise above adversity again and again, and today lives a life of faith and devotion and light. Obstacles and challenges arise in our lives not only to test our strength, but to unveil a greater good that we would never have known if life had been simple and easy. As true as this teaching can be in our private lives, it is even more clear in our efforts and accomplishments in the world at large. Like so many important developments and innovations throughout history, *Escape from Iran* had to rise above difficulty to achieve a greater good.

As the stream of students arriving from Iran to America grew from tens to hundreds to thousands, the expenses and the debt became more and more overwhelming. In the early phases of the program, the initial generosity of the Persian communities in America had made it possible for us to be up and running. As mentioned earlier, at a certain point we felt we had no choice but to turn to the parents of the students and asked them to take some share in covering the costs of this operation, for the Yeshivas, for the teachers, for the classroom and dormitory buildings, for the food and room and board and so on. The results were inadequate to meet a deficit that was skyrocketing toward the two-million-dollar mark.

As one part of a multi-faceted strategy, Rabbi Hecht reached out to the leadership of the Federation of Jewish Philanthropies. We made a presentation to them detailing the very important work we were doing on behalf of these students. It was already running into hundreds of thousands of dollars, we explained, and we requested their support. We were aware of the fact that the Jewish Federation in New York City had never really supported Torah institutions in the metropolitan area. Sadly, they did not change either their philosophy or their modus operandi because of the Iranians. In fact, the Federation went to many of the wealthy Iranians and succeeded in encouraging them to give their support through the Federation, then subsequently only funneled a small percentage of that money back to us. What they did with the rest of those funds is still a mystery. Moreover, when we went to those wealthy Iranian Jews and asked them to contribute, they answered that they had already supported the project through the Federation. There were some individuals among them who, to their very great credit, did offer the financial support we requested. But they were very few. We were also told that a number of the local Iranians were reluctant to help because they felt that since the parents of many of the students were wealthy, they should be carrying the burden of support. We were caught between the hammer and the anvil.

There was also a constituency among the Iranians living in New York who bore a certain resentment toward the Lubavitch community in Brooklyn, inasmuch as we were the ones who had successfully carried out this exodus. Their irrational antipathy showed up in several different ways. One took the form of a group of Iranians in Queens who started a false rumor that the children were not being fed properly—meaning not only that they were not having enough to eat, but also that they were not given homestyle cooking of their own Persian cuisine. So on several occasions, someone would drive up in front of 824 Eastern Parkway and open up the trunk of his car, in which was a pot of rice. They went into the Yeshiva and told the students, "since you are not being served proper Persian food here, we brought you a pot of Persian cooked rice, and there is even *tahdig* at the bottom!" (*Tahdig* is the crisp, crunchy rice at the bottom of the pot.) One or two of the boys probably went out to see the rice, but in essence the whole thing was mostly seen as a joke. Nonetheless, some people did not get the joke and took it seriously, in a very negative way.

Then there was the situation at Lefferts Hospital. Once Rabbi Hecht had gotten over his shock that the building was in shambles, we swiftly began the restoration, bringing in plumbers, electricians, and contractors to fix the rooms and repair the necessary facilities. In the interim, however, some students for whom there was simply no other place moved in there while the construction was still going on, with limited facilities such as showers and toilets. A number of these boys felt very uncomfortable with this, and they expressed as much to their relatives in Queens; or they wrote back to their parents and families in Iran, who then contacted their acquaintances in New York and asked them to check it out.

One of unfortunate results of this was that a group of Iranians in Los Angeles who had no direct access to any information whatsoever heard rumors on top of rumors. They sent a letter to Rabbi Hecht, of blessed memory, in which they expressed their terrible dismay, claiming that the children were being starved, being physically abused, etc., and on and on. The letter was laced with all manner of threats and false innuendoes. This was a sad side effect of the tremendous work that was being done for the children.

There was also an attitude in some circles that since the American Jewish community was so rich, the Rabbis running this program surely had access to millions of dollars to take care of the students. Rabbi Hecht had signed a personal guarantee for every student who arrived in the United States, affirming that he was going to take care of all of their physical needs. Sadly, this backfired, and some students, or their friends, or their families, or other well-intentioned Persians living in the United States told themselves a story about how the organization was raking in millions of dollars and they were hardly giving the kids food. The children were suffering in a building that is in ruins, they claimed, while the Rabbis are getting rich.

This fiction did not affect the day-to-day operations of the schools, nor the lives of the children, nor the ample meals that were being served each day. It is important to state explicitly one thing above all:

that there was always bountiful and plentiful food. Rabbi Hecht, of blessed memory, was a man who always made sure that in every one of the programs and organizations under his aegis, the children were always well fed. And this was especially the case with the students who had come from Iran. Sephardi cooks were hired who were familiar with the cuisine of the Middle Eastern Jews, and they unfailingly created beautiful, abundant meals, always of the highest quality.

Despite all the good that was being accomplished day in, day out, certain bad rumors continued to circulate. There were people in various pockets of the community who harbored a very negative attitude toward the Foreign Student Division and the other schools that had gathered together to serve these children. In particular, the aforementioned complaints coming from Los Angeles turned into a legal battle. Rabbi Hecht hired a law firm in California to employ every legal strategy to stop the attacks by that group against the organization. It took two or three years to resolve the case, but eventually that group did sign a formal letter of apology, in which they acknowledged that all their accusations were false, and based on unsubstantiated rumors. They expressed their profound regret for the terrible problems they had caused. The judge who oversaw the case made sure to levy a punitive fine upon the individuals who had perpetrated the libel.

So these truths were finally confirmed (see letter in the Appendix): (1) that the organization was not raking in any money; (2) though some were living temporarily in a building that had problems, Rabbi Hecht was doing everything to ensure that they would be as comfortable as possible, as soon as possible; (3) the teachers were learned, skilled, devoted to the students, and dedicated to the quality of their work; (4) the cooks were working long hours with heart and soul to prepare delicious Persian food; and (5) everyone in the administration was there not for expediency or personal gain, but out of love and self-sacrifice for the kids.

And the students knew.

# CHAPTER XII
## From the Alborz to the Catskills
൚

*During the two weeks of our initial stay at the Sinai Hotel, Hertzel and I had the opportunity to climb up to the roof for a birdseye view of the city of Tehran. What came to our attention first were the many building cranes stretching from our central vantage point to the outskirts of town—clear signs of a building boom. To the north were the spectacular Alborz Mountains, extending across the horizon from west to east. Tehrani Jews would often vacation in summer homes in villages near Mount Damavand, Iran's highest peak, a symbol of resistance against despotism in Persian poetry, myth, and literature.*

*With summer approaching in Brooklyn,
we too decided to move our students to the
mountains—not to the Alborz, but the Catskills.*

*The Jewish people have a long history of
ascending to the mountaintops for spiritual
illumination.*

*A*s the Iranian students poured into Brooklyn,
the Herculian effort to hire teachers, mentors,
counselors, cooks, maintenance personnel, drivers,
contractors and construction crews continued. With
over 1,000 students under the umbrella of the various agencies Rabbi Hecht supervised by the spring of
1979, we had about 200 on staff. Most of them were
paid; there were also many full-time and part-time
volunteers. It was a massive operation that had an
enormous impact on the entire Crown Heights community as well as on the individuals directly involved.

The never-ending need for more buildings to
house dormitories and classrooms continued to spi-
ral, so we had no choice but to become real estate
*mayvens*. Most of these venues have been mentioned
earlier here and there, but we should consider the
full magnitude of this aspect of the project, our
widespread physical plant:

- In addition to the NCFJE's original building
  at 824 Eastern Parkway, we had more recently

acquired the property next door at 828, which eventually was to be designated as a full-fledged Persian Jewish Center.

- There were two synagogue buildings in East Flatbush. Rabbi Hecht's shul, Yeshiva Meir Simcha Kohen, was used as a starting point for the arriving students, brought there directly from the airport for registration, paperwork, and assignment to residential housing. And two blocks away was the synagogue overseen by Rabbi Michoel Teitelbaum, with its attached classroom building and kitchen.

- As the old Lefferts General Hospital building underwent its urgent repair, it was gradually transformed into another main dormitory facility.

- The **Machon Chana** dorm building on **President Street** housed many of the girls, while others were hosted by families.

- Two other Crown Heights buildings were also repurposed as student residences—the apartment building on the corner of Eastern Parkway and Albany Avenue, and the long-vacant building owned by *Merkos L'Inyanei Chinuch* on Eastern Parkway near Nostrand Avenue.

- The Mott Avenue estate in Far Rockaway, on Jamaica Bay, a property with great potential for a variety of uses, was donated by a group of investors headed by Rabbi Hecht's friend Mr. Irwin Cohen.

That last item on that list wasn't the only contribution made by Mr. Cohen and his associates; nor was it the most significant. Having been made aware of all the difficulties we were going through with respect to dormitory facilities in Brooklyn, and knowing that Rabbi Hecht, of blessed memory, had been a pioneer in establishing Jewish summer camps, the Cohen group came to him in the Spring of 1979 to talk about a property they had in upstate New York.

In the mid-twentieth century—more specifically, in the 1950s—the Catskill Mountains "Borsht Belt" (also affectionately referred to as the "Jewish Alps") boasted some of the most beautiful, lavish, five-star resort hotels in America. Among them was the Esther Manor on Route 17B, near Monticello, New York. In its heyday it was one of the most luxurious hotels; 190 acres on Route 17B, beautiful buildings, indoor and outdoor swimming pools, a small golf course, and all the amenities and luxuries a vacationing "Member of the Tribe" could possibly desire. In the 1970s the whole industry started to take a turn for the worse. At a certain point the property of the Esther Manor was taken over by a group of investors, including Mr. Cohen; and around that time they were approached by an organization that offered special programs for special-needs children. The principal administrators, from a very prominent

Chassidic, Rabbinic family, made a proposal to the investment group, and arranged for the facility to be converted into a school and dormitory for these special-needs kids. The former Esther Manor became the home of the Maimonides Institute.

However, the government funding for this particular type of institution, which included a full-service educational and therapeutic program for the children, came to an end in the late 1970s. Sadly, the owners and Directors of Maimonides decided to close the operations. So the group of investors, who had already gone to great pains to convert the facility to a not-for-profit enterprise, came to Rabbi Hecht in hopes of selling him the property.

Rabbi Hecht, of blessed memory, had an intense, very long meeting with Irwin Cohen and several of his associates in the NCFJE office on Eastern Parkway. Proposals and counter-proposals flew back and forth across the conference table. When they emerged from the meeting, Rabbi Hecht had a radiant smile on his face and announced that an agreement had been reached: to everyone's delight and surprise, the Cohen group had decided to donate the property to the National Committee, as a place of refuge for the Iranian students.

That was how Machaneh Mordechai was born. This huge facility, a once-luxurious resort, was converted into a summer camp for the Iranian boys, renamed in tribute to the great Exilarch Mordechai, righteous leader of the Jewish people during the first Persian exile 2,500 years before. Despite the fact that one of the buildings had been demolished earlier when the property had changed hands, there was enormous potential there.

As always, of course, funds were required to make the necessary reconfiguration and renovations. Leveraging his contacts in Sullivan and Ulster Counties, Rabbi Hecht reached out to the business and Jewish communities of upstate New York, many of whom had prospered mightily during the height of the Borsht Belt boom. A meeting was held at the Concord Hotel, the preeminent hotel at that time, where he made a presentation to the Sullivan and Ulster County Jewish leadership. He requested, on behalf of the children, support for the exodus of Iranian Jewish students to America. The response was enthusiastic, and heartwarming. Donations and pledges of sponsorship for the Machaneh Mordechai facility provided the means to fix the place up to the point where it would be able to accommodate upwards of 400 students and staff. And though the outdoor pool was no longer functional, the indoor pool was brought up to par.

And so it was that in June of 1979, the Yeshiva moved north to Machaneh Mordechai, and the students embarked upon a new lifestyle—part summer camp, part Yeshiva—which continued from June until after the Sukkot holiday of 1979. The educational component was enhanced by the presence of several prominent educators and the assistance of a number of young Rabbinical students. The Iranian boys happily remained in these idyllic surroundings for as long as the weather would permit, until the renovations in the Lefferts Hospital building were approaching completion, when they were able to move back into a comfortable facility upon their return to Brooklyn. Hundreds of Iranian students were housed, fed, attended classes and became acclimated to life in America during that first summer at Machaneh Mordechai. And at the same time, Camp Emunah, our long-standing girls' camp some twenty miles to the east in Greenfield Park, expanded its facilities so as to accommodate the Iranian girls, who were considerably fewer among the refugees than the boys.

Another extraordinary sub-plot to the story of Machaneh Mordechai had to do with the various inspections which would ordinarily have been necessary when reopening a facility which had previously been closed. With the timely assistance of a few influential friends in the region, we were able to prevail upon the local authorities to confer refugee status on our students, and therefore to defer the usual building inspections. After the summer, once the students had returned to New York, those inspections were performed. The result was a substantial list of recommended repairs and alterations which, had they been insisted upon, would probably have shut us down in June. We made the appropriate improvements so that the following summer Machaneh Mordechai was able to operate, not only as a Persian camp, but also as a summer camp for Sephardi children, with many of the Iranian boys attending again. Yet another example of Divine intervention in the guise of a little help from our friends.

Lest anyone imagine that this phase of our work was solely focused on buildings, facilities, and funds, rest assured that these essential efforts to establish the external structures of *Escape from Iran* were all for the sake of permeating the "vessels" with spiritual light and life. We may have been, of necessity, preoccupied much of the time with financial and logistical details. But we never lost sight of the priority: a first-rate education for the young people entrusted to our care, to prepare and empower them for the road ahead.

It was during that time that we made arrangements for Rabbi Eliyahu Ben-Haim to come to the United States. When I was in Iran I had met Rabbi

Eliyahu, an esteemed scholar and educator, the nephew of the venerable *Hacham* Rabbi Netanel Ben-Haim. Rabbi Eliyahu had studied in several Yeshivot in Eretz Yisrael, until his uncle influenced him to come to Iran to serve as a teacher and Rabbi in Tehran. While there I had the privilege of spending quite a bit of time with him discussing matters of Torah study and pedagogy. I came to respect him deeply—his capabilities, his great knowledge, and his expertise as a teacher. As our various school programs had begun to grow, it became evident that we would not only need more teachers, but specifically teachers with mastery in Jewish studies who could speak fluent Farsi. So I began a long distance conversation with Rabbi Eliyahu Ben-Haim, and he agreed to come; he arrived in the States at the end of the summer, in time to move into the Machaneh Mordechai center and join our team. Remaining there until after Sukkot, he then returned with us back to the City to teach in our Brooklyn schools during the following year. Over the next few years, during the summer time, Machaneh Mordechai continued to provide a summer camp setting for the Iranian boys.

Other prominent Rabbis joined our faculty that summer as well, as hundreds more students kept arriving from Iran. The flow continued apace throughout the 1980 school year, by which time the size of the student body was becoming more or less stabilized, because we had begun the process of transferring some students to other schools. Once the number had reached about 1,300 in September of 1979, many of the first waves of students were making contact with relatives, friends, or siblings who had come to America earlier, and they requested to be transferred to other Yeshivot. It wasn't always easy, because the original I-20s designated for our institutions required that they remain for at least six months. But we did our best to honor their choices, and eventually created a system whereby transfers were enabled to several dozen Yeshivot all over the United States, where the students continued their high school or university-level education.

During our second full year of operation, because we were regularly transferring students out to other places, we were averaging approximately 300–400 students in our boys' school, and about 200 female students who were registered in Beis Rivkah and attended various classes in the women's schools in Crown Heights. By June of 1981, the majority of the children had either graduated or successfully transferred to other cities and Yeshivahs. By September of 1981 there was only a small number continuing on in the programs that we had set up. At that point many of those students requested transfers into the existing Yeshivahs in Crown Heights, which meant either Lubavitcher Yeshivah High School, Oholei Torah High School, the central Yeshiva Gedolah housed at 770 Eastern Parkway, or any of several smaller locations in Crown Heights. Over the course of three years, the massive educational initiative we had undertaken for the Iranian refugees had gone from startup to full-throttle to the passing of the baton. That phase of our operation was tapering to a close.

The debts we had incurred, of course, remained to a significant extent unpaid, and were in fact continuing to grow. The repercussions of the heroic efforts of Rabbi Hecht, his loyal staff, and his Board of Directors could be measured in the range of millions of dollars. Even relatively small and unforeseen expenditures—the Bar Mitzvahs and weddings Rabbi Hecht continued to perform and underwrite, for example, for dozens and dozens of young Iranian men and women who had grown up in the community—kept adding up. Unrelenting fundraising campaigns chipped away at the balance sheet, which became gradually (very gradually!) more manageable. Full-page ads were placed in the Anglo-Jewish press. Rabbi Hecht's regularly scheduled radio program and special radiothons elicited the generosity of a widespread audience in the metropolitan area. Eventually the Monticello property and the Far Rockaway properties were sold, which to some degree helped ease the overwhelming debt. The annual banquets, which until then had generally been focused on the ongoing work of the National Committee in all its facets, were concentrated on *Escape from Iran*. Rabbi Moshe Feinstein, the generation's foremost authority on Jewish Law and Rabbinical jurisprudence, wrote a heartfelt letter of support appealing to his worldwide constituency. Though the meetings with and proposals made to New York's Federation of Jewish Philanthropies had proved disappointing, charitable donations from the business and professional communities, largely but by no means exclusively from the Persian Jews, continued to gratify.

## Tefillin for Iran

One of the more fascinating stories that came to light in the course of the Jewish students' escape from Iran involved a transport of a different sort—in this case, not from Iran to America, but the other way around.

Mr. Steven Mukamal, a prominent New York immigration lawyer, had become a dear friend and strong supporter of Rabbi Hecht, of blessed memory, over the years. He was an active member of the NCFJE

## —Rabbi Moshe Feinstein's Letter—

"The importance and influence of the National Committee for Furtherance of Jewish Education, under the leadership of Rabbi Jacob J. Hecht, is well known and appreciated. For several decades Rabbi Hecht had been involved in spreading Torah-true education and has succeeded in saving and bringing close to Torah thousands of Jewish souls, bringing them under the wings of the Divine Presence.

"Recently he has girded himself and undertaken, with great sacrifice, to save the Jewish children in Iran, physically and spiritually. You are no doubt aware of the terrible plight of our Persian Jewish brethren who truly need the great mercy of Heaven, may Hashem protect them and redeem them from the straights of oppression to freedom and redemption from their oppressors, from darkness to great light.

"The Committee has already saved hundreds from the sword and has organized places of refuge, food and shelter and schools, for their education and training in the spirit of our holy Torah. All this has incurred extraordinary financial strain.

"It is a great mitzvah, and it is incumbent upon every member of the Jewish community, our brothers in benevolence of heart, to come and lend support to these heroes and join them in partnership in this great mitzvah of ransoming the captives.

"In this merit may each and every one be blessed with all manner of benevolent blessing . . . for the sake of saving body and soul."

*Rabbi Moshe Feinstein, Lag B'Omer 5739*

Board of Trustees; in fact, he often hosted the organization's Board meetings in his offices in downtown Manhattan. Whenever a problem with someone's green card or citizenship or any other immigration issue would come to Rabbi Hecht's attention, Steve was the man to see. Because of his experience and connections, he was frequently able to iron out major difficulties or leap over seemingly insurmountable roadblocks. Here's how Mr. Mukamal told the story, in the late 1980s—because few people knew about this in the early eighties while it was going on.

After the Ayatollah Khomeini returned to Iran, the Jews became subjugated anew to the Islamic oppression from which they had found refuge during the Shah's more liberal regime. Once again, the Jews became second-class citizens, after the Shah had abdicated and fled. The good relationship and open commerce that had prevailed between Israel and Iran, even in military matters, was over; suddenly there were difficulties in business, in professional life, and in religious observance as well. Israel became the main enemy of Islamic Iran. Khomeini himself was looked upon as the long-awaited Imam who would be the redeemer of all Muslims around the world; the Jews were in the way.

One day a message from Tehran arrived at Rabbi Hecht's office, by way of certain members of the Sephardic Congregation in Queens. It was an urgent request for a hundred pairs of tefillin to be sent to the Jewish community in Iran, if it could possibly somehow be arranged. The Iranian Jews no longer had contact with Israel, so they weren't able to bring in new tefillin or mezuzahs from the customary sources. Rabbi Hecht brought this request to the attention of the Rebbe. The Rebbe encouraged him to figure out a way, but gave no hints as to how; and he added that the Rebbe's office would pay for the tefillin.

Rabbi Hecht sat down to brainstorm with Steve Mukamal. How could they possibly pull off such a far-fetched stunt as to smuggle tefillin into the heart of the Islamic revolution? No Jews in their right mind would dare travel to Iran at that time—it was that dangerous. Suddenly, Steve had a wild idea.

Among the young lawyers working in his office was a female trainee who happened to be the daughter of the Ambassador from Thailand to the United Nations. Steve hatched a plan. He spoke with the young woman and he asked her if she might arrange a meeting for him with her father. No problem, she replied, and before long the Thai Ambassador to the UN and Mr. Mukamal sat down to talk. "We need to bring some religious articles to the Jews of Iran," Steve explained. "It has occurred to me that the only way we might possibly accomplish that would be through a diplomatic pouch."

Diplomatic pouches are sacrosanct. According to internationally accepted guidelines, no one is allowed to open them—they belong to the envoys who bring them, and the host country has no business investigating what they contain. The Ambassador was shown a pair of tefillin, opened up to expose how they are made. The gentleman was very receptive, recognizing this as an opportunity to provide religious assistance to the Jewish people. He left to think it over, discussing the idea, most likely, with others in his diplomatic circle.

He returned to Mr. Mukamal with an agreement and a plan: once the hundred pairs of tefillin were gathered together, they would be sent first to Thailand. From there the diplomatic corps travelling between Bangkok and Tehran would bring a few pairs of tefillin at a time in diplomatic pouches, over the course of several months, until all one hundred pairs reached Tehran.

And so it was. Having seen one set of miracles in the rescue of thousands of students from oppression in Iran, the National Committee managed to make the exodus a two-way street, sending a hundred beams of light back to Iran from the land of Israel by the most circuitous route imaginable. The tefillin arrived in Thailand, were placed in diplomatic pouches and brought to Tehran, and word spread secretly throughout the Jewish community. Every few days the Thai embassy was visited by one or two Jews, ostensibly on diplomatic business, and from there they brought the precious cargo to a synagogue or community center.

Steve Mukamal and Rabbi Hecht, both of blessed memory, loved to tell and retell the story of how, while so many Jewish kids were finding their ways to safety, they had reached deep into the oppressive revolutionary regime and planted in Iran the seeds of mitzvot proclaiming the singular, all-encompassing tenet of the Jewish faith: the oneness of almighty God.

# CHAPTER XIII
## Epilogue
ᔐ

*The Brooklyn Persian Jewish Center was dedicated in May of 1981 at 828 Eastern Parkway, next door to the building that housed the Yeshiva and the NCFJE Headquarters. That year the Passover Seder for the Iranian students took place there for the first time; and as he had done in previous years in the temporary locations, the Rebbe stopped by to visit the students before they began the Seder.*

*After touring the kitchens and dining rooms in both buildings, accompanied by Rabbi Hecht, the Rebbe wished the students a warm and joyous Chag Sameach. Rabbi Hecht then decided to seize the opportunity*

*and escort the Rebbe for a brief visit to the
NCFJE conference room.*

*In the center of the long conference table
there was a beautiful desktop globe. The Rebbe
smiled from ear to ear, gestured toward the
globe, and said to Rabbi Hecht, "I see that you
carry the whole world on your shoulders. Your
good work should spread that far and that
wide." Rabbi Hecht replied, "With the Rebbe's
help, God willing, I can."*

The program of bringing and settling the students continued into 1981. As the thousands of
Iranian Jews we had helped over a three-year period
became increasingly comfortable and well-situated,
the remarkable team of educators and activists the
NCFJE had put together was finally able to find a bit
of respite from the intense, all-consuming, day-and-
night devotion the initial phases of *Escape from Iran*
had required.

Many of the young people who had arrived deepened their relationships with the Crown Heights
community. Some took jobs in bookstores, catering
businesses, and other retail establishments. Some
began to work in various capacities in community
schools. Those who had been pursuing professional
degrees in Iranian universities were able to finish

their college studies in America and move on to their respective professions, some remaining in Crown Heights. Several young men were employed by Mermelstein Caterers, a popular food catering service firm in Crown Heights. Ben Sion Kohen, whom we had first met in Teheran when he volunteered to be our driver, and then worked with us in America counseling the younger students, also worked at Mermelstein's. He soon became a manager there and eventually took over the business, becoming one of the important caterers in Crown Heights. Moshe Chayempour, too, achieved success in the Kosher restaurant and catering business some years later, together with his brothers. Ever-versatile and creative, he had previously put his engineering work to the side to become a professional photographer and videographer. He continues to devote his energies to Jewish community service and activism in Los Angeles.

Many of those who came from Iran to the United States during those years chose to settle in the New York City Borough of Queens, where there was already a strong presence of Sephardim and Persians. Although the Sephardic Congregation of Queens in Forest Hills, where I serve as Rabbi, has catered to families from as many as ten different countries of origin over the years, throughout the 1980s the Persian families in our community predominated among our membership. Our *Hazzan* (Cantor), Mr. Mansour Eliav, though he had grown up in Israel, was originally from Iran, and therefore adept at making special accommodations for the various customs and liturgy of the Iranian community. Other Persian members of our synagogue also spared no effort to welcome the newcomers and help them feel as comfortable and at home as they themselves had come to feel in Queens. And as the Persian community in Queens continued to expand, our members became increasingly involved in the ongoing operations in Brooklyn. Some of the students had relatives in Queens and would come to visit from time to time. My wife, Rebbetzin Channah Hecht, together with Mrs. Zena Abraham and other women of the community, would frequently prepare programs for the Iranian girls; and some of the older Persian college students from our community were there to offer friendship and mentoring. Spearheaded by the Halimi and Moradi families, and many more too numerous to mention here, our shul became a center for extracurricular activities for the students from Crown Heights.

Persian Jewry is blessed with certain distinctive, long-standing, traditional values. Among them is an abiding respect for the spiritual leadership of the *Hacham*—the learned sage and arbiter of Jewish Law.

By the same token there is a very strong and heart-felt recognition of the importance of the synagogue as the center of Jewish life. So wherever members of the Persian community settle, establishing a place for communal activities, learning, and prayer that resonates with their own culture and customs becomes a priority of the first order.

A few years before I went to Iran, Azaria Levy and I had spoken about the possibility of starting a Sephardic/Persian Synagogue in Kew Gardens. After exploring a number of different ideas we decided to approach Rabbi Rosenzweig, the Rabbi of the main synagogue of Kew Gardens, Adath Yeshurun. I was very friendly with Rabbi Rosenzweig—we shared a strong mutual respect and admiration—and I felt certain that he would be sympathetic to the notion of establishing a local Mashhadi congregation on his premises. Years earlier I had assisted in facilitating a similar arrangement with Rabbi Fabian Schoenfeld of the Young Israel of Kew Gardens Hills, initiating a Sephardic *Minyan* there on Shabbat. In fact I had had the great merit during my first decade or so in Queens to help a number of other diverse Sephardi groups find suitable venues for prayer.

Adath Yeshurun was situated in a very large, imposing building, with a young and vibrant mem-bership and many different programs. An agreement was reached whereby the Mashhadi/Persian community of Kew Gardens was permitted to operate a *Minyan* in their building, in a nice-sized room on the basement level, near the Gym. Eventually, the Mashhadi Persian community was able to purchase a property across the street, where they built a beautiful edifice of their own. I remember our discussions concerning the appropriate name for the shul; they decided on the name *Shaarei Tovah*, which means the Gates of Goodness. The *Minyan* grew slowly at first. When we started bringing the Iranian students to America there were quite a few Mashhadi children among them, and before long their parents began to find ways of emigrating from Iran to the United States. There was suddenly a new urgency among the Mashhadis in Kew Gardens. Azaria Levy had been one of the people who supported our original trip to Iran. Now his generosity was coming full circle, welcoming families arriving from Iran and building the Mashhadi community in Queens.

As the community developed, it became time to engage a Rabbi. Rabbi Eliyahu Ben-Haim, the esteemed educator and spiritual leader whom I had first met in Tehran, who had led the Mashhadi Synagogue there, was the perfect candidate—and not only for this role: he was also ideally suited to join the faculty at Machaneh Mordechai and at our Yeshiva in Brooklyn. And so in the late summer of 1979 we were influential in bringing Rabbi Eliyahu Ben-Haim to America, as a teacher in our school and as Rabbi of the Mashhadi community of Kew Gardens. As the years passed, a majority of Mashhadi families migrated to Great Neck, Long Island. Rabbi Ben-Haim eventually was recognized as *Av Bet Din* and also moved to Great Neck, and the community continued to expand there.

The foremost Persian shul in Queens established during that period of time was the Paras Synagogue of Rego Park, just two blocks away from our Sephardic Jewish Center. Rabbi Solomon Dayan, who served as the Rabbi there until his passing, had been a member of our congregation for many years. Another group of our constituents in Queens later moved to Great Neck and established the Ahavat Shalom Synagogue, under the spiritual guidance of Rabbi Isaac Bakhshi. Congregation Ahavat Shalom has taken a strong leadership role there, and it continues to evolve as a very influential presence on Long Island. Great Neck has become a major center of Persian Jewry in the New York area and on the east coast in general, representing of a reawakening of religious life in the Iranian Jewish community in the United States.

A still larger percentage of the community settled in California. Rabbi Yedidia Shofet, formerly considered the Chief Rabbi of Iranian Jewry, emigrated to the United States and established a synagogue in Beverly Hills. His son, Rabbi David Shofet, with whom had we worked closely during the three years when we were bringing the students to America, later took over his father's role. Hertzel Illulian also made his way to Los Angeles, and under his guidance a number of young Rabbis assumed leadership positions throughout the state of California, in community centers, Chabad Houses, and other synagogues. Some had studied at Ner Yisroel in Baltimore; many others had studied in Chabad Yeshivot, including a number of the students who had arrived in Brooklyn in 1978. The dynamic presence of the Persian community continues to flourish on both coasts.

The educational opportunities both New York and California provide, with their first-rate Day Schools and Yeshivot and their thriving Jewish culture, have rendered the level of knowledge, observance, and community involvement among newly arrived Persian Jews significantly more robust than when they were in Tehran—perhaps even greater than throughout many centuries in exile.

Meanwhile in Crown Heights, where *Escape from Iran* had first taken hold, many Iranian emigres decided to remain or return there. Given the presence of a growing Persian community, it became evident that there was a need for a Persian synagogue in Crown Heights. Although we had been careful in our schools to encourage the Iranian students to maintain their traditional liturgy and other customs, nonetheless the community at large followed Chabad practices. The Persians deserved a center of their own.

Rabbi Hecht was at the forefront of this, as in many other things. The buildings at 824–828 Eastern Parkway had been renovated numerous times to accommodate the new students with dorm and classrooms; on the second floor of 828 there were still several rooms that could be converted into a nice size synagogue with both men's and women's sections. The construction was begun without delay.

The members of our congregation in Forest Hills who had already generously sponsored our work, from the original trip to Iran through the ongoing developments in America, took a keen interest in this new project. I had frequently mentioned aspects of our operations in my sermons on Shabbat to keep people apprised of our progress; many of our friends found the new Persian synagogue particularly exciting. One of the first considerations was the question of to whom the shul should be dedicated. It was roundly agreed that it would be most appropriate to honor the memory of Mr. Habib Elghanian, who had been the first martyr assassinated by the Khomeini regime two years before. Mr. Elghanian's son, Sina, had attended the Sephardic Congregation during the year that he was saying Kaddish for his father, so there was a close relationship between our community and the Elghanian family. Sina was approached about the proposal, and after some negotiation and discussion he agreed to take upon himself to dedicate the synagogue in memory of his father. As the finishing touches on the renovations were finalized, plans for the special dedication event, the *Hanukat Habayit*, were already underway.

At the same time we embarked upon the writing of a *Sefer Torah* especially for the Persian children and families. We spread the word in the community, asked people to participate by purchasing a letter in the *Sefer Torah*, and decided to celebrate the *Hachnasat Sefer Torah* at that same *Hanukat Habayit* event. My wife, Rebbetzin Channah Hecht, was intensely involved in planning the program, as were many members of our congregation in Queens. A partial list of the key participants included Mr. Halimi, Mr. and Mrs. Yehuda Abraham, the Moradi family, Mr. and Mrs. Sabett, and Mr. Mayer Abraham. The Crown Heights community was also well represented, in particular by Mr. and Mrs. Sam Malamud and Mr. and Mrs. Shaya Boymelgreen. Both families had adopted Iranian girls into their homes, and had been active in creative projects to help the Persian girls in Crown Heights, as well as various fundraising initiatives.

The Dedication was held in March of 1981. Rabbi Hecht delivered an impassioned sermon about the Persian Jews and the power of prayer in the Beit HaKnesset. Hazzan Mansour Eliav, cantor of the Sephardic Congregation of Queens, led the services; Moshe Chayempour said a few words; Aziz Halimi was asked to serve as auctioneer and auction off the various honors. Then the Sefer Torah was placed in the *Aron Kodesh*. Sinai Elghanian was given an opportunity to speak in memory of his father, as a *Kadosh*—a martyr not only in the eyes of the Iranian Jewish community but among Jews all over the world. Amidst great joy, honor, and respect, the synagogue was dedicated in the name of Habib Elghanian as the Persian Jewish Center of Brooklyn.

To the many members of the Crown Heights community in attendance who had devoted themselves to arrival and education of the Iranian students, and to the Persians who came from Queens and Long Island, and especially to those families who had settled in Crown Heights, the Dedication was seen as a major leap forward in the establishment of the Persian community in their new homeland.

Over the years the Crown Heights Center has remained a Sephardic congregation, with predominantly Persian Jews in attendance. Some of the original students who came in 1978 and 1979 are still active, enthusiastic members who care deeply for the upkeep and growth of the shul. As one of the first new institutions designated for Persian Jewry in America, the Center was a tremendous accomplishment, another step in the ongoing redemption from *galut Bavel/Paras*, now free to flourish in the United States.

Three months later, on the third anniversary of the martyrdom of Habib Elghanian, we held a memorial *Azkara* meal in the synagogue named in his honor, paying due respect to the memory of a man who had embodied the spirit of Persian Jewry and had given his life *Al Kiddush Hashem*. The well-attended event was observed with inspirational words of Torah, speeches by various dignitaries, the installation of a handsome plaque in the shul, and a beautiful commemorative meal in our Machon Chana school across the street at 825 Eastern Parkway. The Elghanian family all participated, including Mr. John Elghanian, brother of Habib Elghanian and one of the prominent leaders of the Iranian Jewish community in the United States. He was also among those deeply involved in the entire process of bringing the children to the United States. Mr. Elghanian's sister, Parvaneh Assil, was also in attendance; she had often come to Brooklyn along with members of her own family to be of help to the newly arrived students in the United States. The family continued in their support of the work of the National Committee on behalf of the Persian community.

## Pesach in Pakistan, and Other Roads to Redemption

Once the students were becoming settled in and acclimated to life in the United States, families who had remained in Iran began to realize that a channel had been opened. Perhaps it would be possible to relocate themselves. For the Persian Jews, however, this was not a simple aspiration to embrace. There had been a continuous presence of Jews there for thousands of years. There was tremendous pride associated with their tradition and history; Persia was home to the burial places of many great *tzadikim* and prophets of antiquity, including Mordechai and Esther, the Prophet Daniel, and others dating back to the era between the first and second Temples.

Suddenly there was great upheaval in the land. The relative tranquility during the reign of Shah Pahlevi had not been ideal by any means—the Jews were considered *dhimmis*, second-class citizens—but still, they were the People of the Book, and protected. Then came the revolution and the demonic Islamist leaders who had begun to terrorize the Jewish community with forced conscriptions, abductions, and worse. It became painfully clear that the 2,500 years of Jewish presence in Iran may well be coming to an end. They began to consider ways of resettling outside of Iran. Some had become wealthy, in many cases via their connections with the oil industry during the years when Iran was in a position of leadership in OPEC. But the Shah himself had indicated to the Jews that as much as he appreciated their loyalty, he couldn't guarantee their safety. So those who had the means to do so sought out ways to transfer their wealth to other countries, even during the good times. This became increasingly difficult with the passage of time.

After the US embassy was overrun, the Israeli embassy shut down. Initially people panicked to get on the last few EL AL flights. The situation was serious enough that the Israeli airline was directed to take any Jews who could get on the planes, with or without tickets or papers. Then things calmed down a bit, to no small degree due to the NCFJE's program for rescuing Iranian Jewish students; the priority became getting the kids out of the country. But before long the families themselves began to realize that they too would have to find ways of escaping Iran. Obtaining visas to the US went from difficult to impossible, even when attempting to apply for religious refugee status. The Iranian government was willing to grant the children student visas so long as their families remained, but once the families began to leave, the whole process first slowed, then ground to a halt. Many early escapees were able to get to Europe, Italy or England, as their kids had done, or to Austria, and from there apply for asylum in America. Asylum was generally granted, although sometimes only after months of waiting, if they brought documentation that they were Jews who had been oppressed. Eventually they would apply for green cards and citizenship of the United States. But there came a time when the gates to Europe slammed shut in Iran.

At that point the only viable option was to travel by land. Arrangements were made for caravans to take Jewish families through Afghanistan and Pakistan, either on the backs of camels or in caravans of trucks. Once in Pakistan, they would make their way to the large cities in the south, and from there they would either get a boat or find a way to book air travel from Pakistan to Austria, or to Italy, and then on to their final destination in the United States.

In 1986, a large group of these refugees had left Iran for Pakistan, but the trip took a little longer than planned and they arrived a week or so before Passover. They sent a message to their family members who attended my synagogue in Queens, saying that they were stuck in Pakistan and would have to remain there during the holiday of Pesach. Could someone possibly make arrangements for them to receive Matzoh and kosher wine in Pakistan, so that they would be able to observe the *Sedarim*?

The word "impossible" was not part of the vocabulary of Rabbi Jacob J. Hecht, of blessed memory. He got to work right away, first consulting with the Rebbe, while beginning to formulate a plan. One of the senior rabbinical students, Zalman Gerber, who had a fair amount of experience traveling to different countries—sometimes under adverse circumstances— was approached. Asked if he would undertake this important and dangerous mission, he did not exactly jump at the opportunity, but he realized that it had to be done and accepted the mission. Through our friends in the Iranian Jewish communities we were able to establish contacts so that he could get a visa as a rug merchant, and he prepared for his trip. The Matzoh was packed into his suitcases, along with non-alcoholic grape juice, and he set out on his flight to Karachi, Pakistan. In order to get through customs, he had planned to explain that he was on a restricted diet, that he needed these distinctive breads and could only eat these special crackers. Miraculously, when the suitcases were opened, no one even asked about the Matzoh. The custom officials studied the Hebrew words on the Matzoh boxes, did not ask any questions, and waved him through. The large quantity of grape juice was probably a little harder to explain, but so long as it wasn't wine they were okay with it. He passed easily through customs.

He made his way to the hotel where it had been prearranged that he would meet with the group that had been stuck in Pakistan. He showed them the Matzoh and grape juice, and together they scrambled to gather up whatever other foods they could find that were kosher for Pesach. It was decided that they would use two of the rooms in the hotel for the Seder so as to make it more likely that they would go unnoticed. They certainly didn't want to draw attention to themselves by going to some central location outside the hotel. So they opted for a decentralized Seder, conducted by the young man from Brooklyn. He first went to one of the rooms where there were a few dozen people. They went through the Seder by the book, distributing the Matzoh piece by piece to each and every person, saying the blessings on the four cups of grape juice, and recounting the story of our exodus from the slavery and oppression of ancient Egypt.

Then he went to another room, where a somewhat despondent group of the younger refugees had gathered. They were feeling that the community leader who had left Iran with them had actually abandoned them, having received his own travel permit and left Karachi before Passover. Distributing the matzoh and the wine, performing the Seder again for them, Zalman instilled in them a renewed feeling of hope and faith. He successfully celebrated the Seder on both nights of Passover with all the Persian Jews who had been marooned that Pesach in Pakistan.

After the first days of the holiday he returned to the United States and reported on the accomplishment of his mission to Rabbi Hecht and to the Rebbe. Eventually those Jews who had been caught in Pakistan for Pesach were able to get travel documents, arrange for tickets, and find their circuitous way to the United States, having experienced their own personal liberation from bondage—their exodus from the oppression of a modern-day Egypt in Iran.

Arriving in America is hardly the long-awaited return to the Promised Land. Not quite, and not yet. But for the Jewish community of Iran, as it has been for so many persecuted Jews escaping from warring regimes in these modern times, finding refuge and creating a new home in the "Land of the Free" has been a major step in the right direction. If we look back at the state of Persian Jewry in 1978, and think about the turn of events that took place following our first visit to Iran, we can clearly see the benevolent hand of Divine Providence.

## Final Thoughts

Hidden within the bitterness of exile are the seeds of revelation and redemption. We can see this in the Biblical history of our Exodus from Egypt, and in our personal lives as well, though it may not be apparent to us during the hard times. And often the route is indirect, with many unforeseen twists and turns. During the early months of the operation, when we had a few hundred students in New York, we began to realize that the time would come when the general Iranian Jewish community would be seeking salvation, and would perhaps seek the route of Exodus out of Iran. My father brought this point to the Rebbe's attention and asked for his advice.

At that point in time we were still in the experimental stages and our programs were not yet fully developed. The dorms and schools had not yet been firmly established; everything was still in flux. The Rebbe suggested that Rabbi Hecht advise families

seeking to emigrate that it would be wiser to make
aliya to Israel, rather than to come to the United
States. He mentioned to my father that in Israel
there would be fewer problems in Kashrut, Shabbat,
etc. At the same time, the Rebbe continued to urge
my father to bring all the students who were leaving
Iran on I-20 visas to New York, to become part of the
operation that was evolving in Brooklyn under the
auspices of Chabad.

Throughout the twentieth century we had seen
a steady flow of Aliya to Israel from Iran. In the late
1960s, for example, my wife and I lived in Kiryat
Malachi as part of the founding Kollel members of
*Nachalat Har Chabad*, which became the Lubavitch
settlement in Kiryat Malachi. There we befriended
many residents who were members of the Persian
community that had settled in Kiryat Malachi just
after 1948. They still lived in the wooden bungalows
to which they had been assigned when they arrived.
They were devoted and loyal Jews; their sons joined
the Israel Defense Forces, and they were very proud
members of Israeli society. They had become shop-
keepers, professionals, and elected officials.

The concept of Aliya was not new to the Persian
community. Many of those who left Iran and went
to Israel were successfully absorbed in the new State
of Israel, despite having come to Israel without any

financial support whatsoever. They found ample opportunities in the Holy Land to start from scratch and establish their lives anew.

In the 1980s the situation was quite different. When the Iranian community began to look for new homes, Israel remained a very important option. But Europe was another; and now, suddenly, America was opening up—especially for those whose sons and daughters had been brought to America through our program, given a good education, and had settled in as American residents who would eventually get visas, green cards and citizenship. The idea of coming to the United States was beginning to be seen as an increasingly attractive opportunity.

As it worked out, the vast majority of the *galut Bavel* who emigrated from Iran in the 1980s did come to the United States. The reestablishment of the Iranian Jewish community took hold on the fertile soil of America, complemented by the thousands of young men and women who were receiving a proper Jewish education and effective orientation. In no small part this was because we had done our best to provide the children with not only a proper secular education, but also with a basic Jewish education in our schools, as well as in all the other schools to which they were transferred during our first three years in operation.

So from a historical perspective, the work of bringing the students to the United States on I-20 visas will go down in history as the game changer. With the help of the framework we established, with the assistance of many other Jewish organizations, and with the invaluable, hard-won support of the United States State Department in conferring refugee status, a tidal wave of emigration transferred the 2,500-year-old diaspora of Paras/Iran to the shores of a new world. In the United States they were able to put down proper roots, build Jewish communities, create beautiful synagogues and congregations, and establish the strong Jewish schools necessary to provide a proper Jewish education for the Iranian Jewish children in America.

Hertzel Ilulian's dream of going to Iran to strengthen traditional Torah-true observance came full circle. It was here in the United States that the Jewish Iranian immigrants reestablished the Iranian diaspora, with its strong historical heritage of *Yehudei Paras*, on a much more resilient foundation than had been experienced for hundreds of years. Looking back after these years, studying the many varied enclaves of Persian Jews with their dozens of synagogues and schools, we have to say that the effort that began as an experiment, created and nurtured by Rabbi Hecht under the direction of the

Lubavitcher Rebbe, has matured and grown into one of the most extraordinary segments of American Jewry. It is without doubt a breathtaking tribute to the history and heritage of Iranian Jews.

It is essential that the second and third generations of Iranian Jews born in the United States be aware of the forces, the sacrifices, and the intense effort involved in providing the framework for the establishment of Iranian Jewry in the United States. It is very important that the chronicle of these accomplishments be passed on through the generations. History will mark this time as a key period of transition, in which the *galut Bavel*, which had begun with the destruction of the first Beit HaMikdash, culminated in the transfer of the communities that had arisen out of First Temple Jewry into the new world of America.

We were fortunate that Divine Providence chose us to be an important part of the establishment and development of the framework in which this segment of World Jewry will continue to flower, blossom, and grow, as we draw closer to the coming of our righteous Moshiach.

Stepping back to see the big picture, it can be said that Khomeini's terrible revolution actually served to save the quality of Jewish life in the Iranian Jewish community. Under our Rebbe's leadership,

Rabbi Jacob J. Hecht guided a group of truly devoted workers who paved the way for a new Exodus, transplanting the pride and glory of Persian Jewry on American shores. And our mission and our story are not yet done.

# Appendix
ᘒ

## Jewish Council for Social and Cultural Advancement

P. O. Box 1771
TEHERAN, IRAN.

Date    Oct, 1, 1978

Mr.   Hekht

Lubavitch World Headquarters
770 Eastern Parkway
Brooklyn, N.Y. 11213

Dear Mr. Hekht

We would like to thank you very much for your kind cooperation
with out center during your visit from Tehran.

Following your discussion with our Mr. Sabzerou regarding extention
our Jewish Library, we would like to ask you to inform us your
possibilities to help us—by sending related lists and books.

Thanking you for your kind attention and looking forward for your
reaction,
dear sir, we remain
with best wishes for zion.

Fereydoun Ghatan

Director

B"H

HADAR HATORAH - FOREIGN STUDENTS

AFTERNOON SCHEDULE - SECOND SEMESTER Beginning Feb. 25

| SUNDAY | MONDAY | TUESDAY | WEDNESDAY | THURSDAY | FRIDAY |
|---|---|---|---|---|---|
| 1:00 -4:30 | 1:30-3:45 | 1:00-1:45 | 1:00-3:45 | 1:00-4:00 | NO |
| English I | English I | Yahadus I | English I | English I | C l a s s e s |
| Mr. Teitelman | Mr. Teitelman | Rabbi Reizes Rm: 202 -------------- | Mr. Teitelman | Mr. Teitelman | |
| Rm:208 | Rm: 208 | Yahadus II Rabbi Katz Rm: 211 | Rm: 208 | Rm: 208 | |
| English II | English II | 1:45-2:00 | English II | English II | Have A NICE AND PLEASANT S H A B B O S |
| Mrs. Weils | Mrs. Weils | MINCHA | Mrs. Weils | Mrs. Weils | |
| Rm: 211 | Rm: 211 | | Rm: 211 | Rm: 211 | |
| English III | English III | 2:00 | English III | English III | |
| Mrs. Gutnick | Mrs. Gutnick | Special Program | Mrs. Gutnick | Mrs. Gutnick | |
| Rm: 202 | Rm: 202 | Everyone must participate | Rm: 202 | Rm: 202 | |
| 4:45-5:00 | 3:45-4:00 | | | 3:45-4:00 | 4:15 |
| MINCHA | MINCHA | | | MINCHA | MINCAH |
| 5:00-5:45 | 4:00-5:30 | | | 4:00-5:30 | 4:30-5:15 |
| Yahaduth I | Physical | | | Physical . | Yahaduth I |
| Rabbi Reizes Rm: 202 ------------ | Ed. | | | Ed. | Rabbi Reizes Rm: 202 ------------ |
| Yahadut II | | | | | Yahadut II |
| Rabbi Katz Rm: 211 | | | | | Rabbi Katz Rm: 211 |

SUPPER 6:15
Arvit 7:00

HADAR HATORAH - FOREIGN STUDENTS

MORNING SCHEDULE - SECOND SEMESTER - Beginning Feb. 25

| 9:15 - 10:00 | 10:00 -10:45 | 11:00 -11:45 | 11:45-12:15 | |
|---|---|---|---|---|
| TORAH III<br>RABBI KATZ<br>Rm 211 | ·MISHNA III<br>RABBI KATZ<br>Rm: 211 | HEBREW III<br>MR. AMAR<br>Rm: 202 | HALACHA III<br>RABBI KATZ<br>Rm: 211 | LUNCH |
| TORAH II<br>RABBI REIZES<br>Rm: 202 | MISHNAH II<br>RABBI REIZES<br>Rm: 202 | HEBREW II<br>MR. GAL<br>Rm: 211 | HALACHA II<br>RABB'<br>CARLEBACH<br>Rm: 202 | LUN_H |
| TORAH I<br>RABBI<br>CARLEBACH<br>Rm  208 | MISHNA I<br>RABBI<br>CARLEBACH<br>Rm: 208 | SPECIAL<br>CLASS<br>RABBI REIZES<br>Rm: 201 | HALACHA I<br>RABBI REIZES<br>Rm: 201 | LUNCH |
| | SPECIAL<br>CLASS<br>Rm: 206 | SPECIAL<br>CLASS<br>Rabbi<br>CARLEBACH<br>Rm: 206 | | LUNCH |

# EXODUS 1980
## WILL IT EVER HAPPEN IN IRAN?

While the world waits in anticipation of the freedom of American hostages with a feeling of despair and virtual abandonment, we Jews are still engulfed with a sense of true belief and confidence in the almighty that he can and will assist us in saving our brethren around the world. The NCFJE is the only organization which has been responsible for the actual evacuation of more than 1,000 Iranian Jewish youth in the past year and which is still actively engaged in such activities on a major international scale.

**EXODUS 1979**

Last year a dramatic air-lift "immigration operation" brought 992 Iranian Jewish youngsters to New York and freedom. They were cared for, educated, housed and fed for extended periods of time. Some were transferred on their request to other educational facilities and others remained for extended periods of time in Crown Heights either housed in dormitory facilities or private homes. In all cases they were financially subsidized by the National Committee.

After the transfer of approximately 300 of these students which required the assistance of the NCFJE to reach the prearranged specific destination our organization fulfilled its obligation of caring for the remainder of students.

**HOME AND HOPE, TO 600+ YOUNG IRANIAN JEWS, IS THE NCFJE**

They were not cold statistics. They were uprooted young children and teenagers who were depending on the NCFJE for love, care, shelter and a proper Jewish education. They came to us with hopes and dreams, seeking to enjoy the freedom and opportunities we in America too often take for granted. The NCFJE willingly accepted the burden and challenge of this noble cause. We did not let them down.

**SPECIAL TEACHERS, SPECIAL PROGRAMS**

Anticipating the special needs of our young Iranian wards, the NCFJE called upon the expertise of its two internationally-acclaimed educational facilities, Hadar Hatorah for Boys and Machon Chana for Girls, to rapidly organize a staff and curriculum for the first complete Iranian Yeshiva in the U.S.

To overcome the language barrier, as most of the young Iranians could neither speak nor read English or Hebrew, we hired accredited associate professors and high-school level teachers who specialize in language. The success of this high-priority program is how evidenced in the fact that several of our original 46 students are now speaking English and Hebrew fluently, and have entered into the mainstream of a regular High School Program.

Taking steps to meet the needs of our vastly expanded student body, ranging in age from 10 to 21, we added an Elementary and Post-High-School program to our regular curriculum. Thus all of the youngsters were able to follow through with their original academic plans in addition to enjoying the benefits of their Torah studies.

**A WHOLESOME JEWISH ENVIRONMENT**

With love and care, as "parents pro tem," the NCFJE provided a proper home for all of our Iranian youngsters. Many of the boys were being housed in our recently acquired Foreign Students Building, in dormitories which have been remodelled and boast all-new furniture carefully chosen for comfort as well as function.

At that time, as we did not have available facilities for all, some of the boys and the young women were being housed by families who were being paid a monthly stipend by the NCFJE and Lubavitch movement. Naturally all homes selected were carefully investigated beforehand to make sure that a proper Jewish home environment and warm-hearted welcome awaited the youngster.

**THE LABORS OF LOVE**

Before the Passover holidays, the NCFJE purchased and converted Brooklyn's Lefferts General Hospital into a comfortable, fully-equipped dormitory for the Iranian youth.

The NCFJE established, constructed, equipped and staffed CAMP MORDECHAI, providing some 400 Iranian youngsters a summer of fun in a wholesome Jewish atmosphere.

From August through January 1980, the NCFJE assisted approximately 425 of these 600 students in settling with families and relatives in 40 communities around the U.S.

During that same period, I, NCFJE placed Iranian high school students in some 40 Yeshivoth and Torah Institutes where they are now learning, and aided over 100 others in transferring to many major universities.

MIRRER YESHIVAH-YESHIVAH CHAIM BERLIN-TELZ YESHIVAH-BAIS YAAKOV-MARYLAND HEBREW THEOLOGICAL COLLEGE (SKOKIE)-HEBREW ACADEMY OF GREATER WASHINGTON-YESHIVAH OF LONG BEACH CALIFORNIA-TALMUDIC ACADEMY OF BALTIMORE-BAIS YAAKOV-BROOKLYN-NER ISRAEL INSTITUTE-SEATTLE-HEBREW ACADEMY-YESHIVAH OR ELCHONON CHABAD-LOS ANGELES-HILLEL ACADEMY-PITTSBURGH-HEBREW ACADEMY OF NEW ENGLAND-JUDAIC COLLEGE-CHICAGO-YESHIVAH OF HUDSON COUNTY, N.J.-BAIS YEHUDAH-DETROIT EMEK YESHIVAH-L.A.-YESHIVAH DAY SCHOOL-PROVIDENCE, R.I.-YESHIVAH DOV REVEL-QUEENS, N.Y. EZRA ACADEMY-QUEENS, N.Y. YESHIVAH HIGH SCHOOL OF QUEENS-BAIS YAAKOV OF QUEENS-HEBREW ACADEMY OF WEST QUEENS-YESHIVOTH HAICHAL HATORAH-BROOKLYN-MESIFTA OF LONG BEACH, N.Y. RAMBAM TORAH INSTITUTE (CALIFORNIA)-HEBREW ACADEMY OF HUDSON COUNTY-YESHIVAH HIGH SCHOOL FOR GIRLS-LONG BEACH, CALIFORNIA-BRISCOE JEWISH HIGH SCHOOL, MASS. YESHIVAH-ATLANTA, GEORGIA NEW HAVEN HEBREW DAY SCHOOL-YESHIVAH SAMSON RAPHAEL HIRSH-N.Y. ACHAI TMIMIM-WORCESTER, MASS. SHAAREI TORAH-MONSEY, N.J. SEATTLE HEBREW ACADEMY-FRISH ACADEMY-N.J. UNITED LUBAVITCHER YESHIVOTH-HADAR HATORAH RABBINICAL SEMINARY-YESHIVAH UNIVERSITY-N.Y.

**WHERE DO WE GO FROM HERE?**

At this writing, 175 Iranian Jewish youngsters are still being cared for by the NCFJE, being fed, clothed, housed in a proper wholesome Jewish environment, attending Hadar Hatorah, Machon Chana, Beth Rivkah and Lubavitch schools, to gain a Torah-true education.

**EXODUS 1980 HAS JUST BEGUN**

The turmoil in Iran continues unabated. And more families are asking for assistance in sending their children to us. And, again, we cannot refuse. This new work has begun and is being done by the NCFJE, and will continue until all Iranian Jews have been evacuated, despite the fact that we are facing staggering expenses, debts, and deficits.

**SHARING IN OUR MITZVAH**

Although we consider it a privilege to care for the Iranian youth we are forced to share this Mitzvah with our fellow Jews. With expenses in the past year exceeding $1,800,000 and income from fund raising, grants and some tuition and immigration fees of some $640,000, the NCFJE is suffering from a massive deficit and credit crunch, critical to its actual existence.

**AN URGENT PLEA FOR ACTION**

More children. There is an urgent need to provide the matzohs, wines, and special foods for Passover 1980. The NCFJE asks you to demonstrate your love and compassion for our Jewish Iranian Children... to help us make their PASSOVER a time they will forever remember as the time they fellow Jews said "We care, we love you and we want to help"!

ב"ה

به نام خــــدا

آقایان و پسرها (۱۳سالببالا)
هر روز هفته بغیرا زروزشبات
وموعدها وتعتیلات مختلف ——
تفیلین ببندید .

بــــراخـــاهـــای تفیلمــسین

## The Board for Persian
## Speaking Students

770 Eastern Parkway
Brooklyn, New York 11213
Tel.: 778-4270 or 756-1117

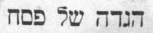

# הגדה של פסח

תורגם ע״י

יהושע נתנאלי

## هگادا شل پسح

ترجمه از یهوشوع نتنالی

## چاپ دوم

چاپ و انتشار توسط هزرهتوراه
و معاون سهبا (حشر داشئون سعاسعی)

Published by
HADAR HATORAH FOREIGN STUDENT DIVISION

NATIONAL COMMITTEE FOR THE FURTHERANCE OF JEWISH EDUCATION
Rabbi Jacob J. Hecht, Executive Vice President
1979

**RABBI MOSES FEINSTEIN**
**455 F. D. R. DRIVE**
**New York 2, N. Y.**
—
ORegon 7-1222

משה פיינשטיין
ר"מ תפארת ירושלים
בנוא יארק

בע"ה

הנה כבר ידוע ומפורסם גודל החשיבות של "ועד החינוך הכשר" תחת הנהלת
הרב ר' יעקב יהודה העכט שליט"א שזה עשיריות בשנים שעוסק בהפצת חינוך
על טהרת הקודש וב"ה הצליח להציל ולקרב אלפי נפשות מאחב"י והכניסם
תחת כנפי השכינה. וזה לא זמן רב אשר אזר חלציו וקבל עליו במסירת
נפש נפלאה להציל את אחב"י המצויים בסעהראן ילדי פרס, הן בגשמיות
והן ברוחניות.

בטח מוכר לכל את מגורל הנורא של אחב"י באיראן, אשר זקוקים הם לרחמי
שמים מרובים. ה' יגין עליהם ויוציאם מן המיצר אל המרחב, מאפילה לאור
גדול ומחח נוגשיהם. והנה הועד הנ"ל כבר הצליח להציל מאות פליטי
חרב אלו והכין להם מקום לאש"ל וסידר להם מקומות חינוך והדרכה עפ"י
רוח תורה"ק.

וכל זה עולה לסכום עצום, ומצוה וחוב קדוש על כאו"א מאחב"י נדיבי לב
לבא בעזרת ה' בגבורים, ולהיות שותף במצוה גדולה זו של פדיון שבויים.
ובזכות זה יתברך כאו"א בכל מילי דמיטב.

STEPHEN J. SOLARZ
13th District, New York

COMMITTEES:
INTERNATIONAL RELATIONS
POST OFFICE AND
CIVIL SERVICE

WASHINGTON OFFICE:
MICHAEL LEWAN
ADMINISTRATIVE ASSISTANT
1530 Longworth House Office Building
Washington, D.C. 20515
(202) 225-2361

**Congress of the United States**
**House of Representatives**
**Washington, D.C. 20515**

DISTRICT OFFICES:
KENNETH LOWENSTEIN
DISTRICT REPRESENTATIVE
1828 Kings Highway
Brooklyn, New York 11229
(212) 965-5100
117 Brighton Beach Avenue
Brooklyn, New York 11235
(212) 965-5105

December 14, 1979

Rabbi Jacob Hecht
824 Eastern Parkway
Brooklyn, NY 11213

Dear Rabbi Hecht:

Enclosed is a copy of a letter I received today from the Acting Commissioner of the Immigration and Naturalization Service which I know will be of interest to you regarding the Iranian students.

I had a meeting with the Commissioner on Wednesday in my office. He was most reassuring in his comments, saying that no Jew would be deported and asked if we knew of any problems to get in touch with him immediately.

There is a backlog of asylum cases, as you may know, and one can expect a wait of at least several months before having an asylum hearing. His statistics indicated that over 400 students have requested asylum at the moment, but he expects the numbers to climb.

Please do not hesitate to get in touch with me or Mike or Dawn if you run into any problems regarding Iranians-- either trying to get into the U.S. or avoid deportation.

Cordially,

STEPHEN J. SOLARZ
Member of Congress

SJS:dc/g

Enclosure

UNITED STATES DEPARTMENT OF JUSTICE
IMMIGRATION AND NATURALIZATION SERVICE
WASHINGTON, D.C.  20536

PLEASE ADDRESS REPLY TO

DEC 1 3 1979

AND REFER TO THIS FILE NO

OFFICE OF THE COMMISSIONER

CO 703.1238

Honorable Stephen J. Solarz
House of Representatives
Washington, D.C.    20515

Dear Mr. Solarz:

This is in response to your letter to the President regarding the
immigration status of Iranian minority groups presently in the United
States.

The policy in effect with regard to the deportation of Iranians is
directed toward those who are here in an unlawful status.  Those Iranians
who are observing a lawful immigration status will not have such status
terminated.  Those who are in an unlawful immigration status and are
unable or unwilling to return to Iran because of a well founded fear of
persecution based on race, religion or political opinion may apply for
asylum before, during or after deportation proceedings are instituted.
A request for asylum made prior to institution of deportation proceedings
will be treated as a confidential matter and no information will be
released to the general public.  However, asylum requests made after
deportation proceedings are instituted cannot be treated as a confidential
matter since deportation hearings are open to the public.  By having
each individual make application for asylum, rather than designate
a particular group or groups for a preferential grant of asylum, adverse
repercussions toward members of these groups in Iran will be minimized.

Work permits will be issued to those Iranians who establish a prima
facie case for asylum and who are financially unable to maintain themselves while in the United States.  Those Iranians who are observing a
lawful student status may apply in the normal manner for permission to
work part-time where economic need is established.

Sincerely,

David Crosland
Acting Commissioner

STEPHEN J. SOLARZ
13TH DISTRICT, NEW YORK

COMMITTEES:
FOREIGN AFFAIRS
CHAIRMAN, SUBCOMMITTEE ON AFRICA
BUDGET

### Congress of the United States
### House of Representatives
### Washington, D.C. 20515

WASHINGTON OFFICE:
1536 LONGWORTH HOUSE OFFICE BUILDING
WASHINGTON, D.C. 20515
(202) 225-2361

DISTRICT OFFICES:
1818 KINGS HIGHWAY
BROOKLYN, NEW YORK 11229
(212) 965-5100

155 BRIGHTON BEACH AVENUE
BROOKLYN, NEW YORK 11235
(212) 965-5100

July 28, 1981

Rabbi Jacob Hecht
824 Eastern Parkway
Brooklyn, NY 11213

Dear Rabbi Hecht:

Knowing of your deep concern for the thousands of Iranians who have taken refuge in our country, I wanted you to know that I learned recently that the State Department has begun to process the 9,000 asylum applications filed by Iranians.

Under our law, each case must be carefully screened first by the State Department to determine if the person's application documents the need for asylum and a further screening by the Immigration and Naturalization Service. If an asylum application is considered incomplete, the applicant should be notified by INS and asked to supply additional information. This request is not a cause for any alarm, as the law requires individual consideration of every asylum request, and also provides for appeals of unfavorable decisions. INS District Directors are given considerable discretion in approving asylum requests and will, I am sure, instruct their officers to proceed with great care on asylum cases.

As you know, our Refugee Act specifically forbids the deportation of any alien, except for serious cause such as fraud or criminal acts, to a country when the Attorney General determines that his or her life or freedom would be threatened because of race, religion, nationality, membership in a particular social group, or political opinion.

In the next month the State Department should refer about 1,000 requests filed in 1979 to INS for further processing and interviews. If any problems arise in the treatment of these applications, which are confidential, I would appreciate your contacting me immediately. I have assigned Dawn Calabia on my staff in Washington and Sylvia Wurf in the District (965-5100) to follow these important asylum requests, and please do not hesitate to contact them.

-2-

    I am also enclosing a copy of the State Department's human rights report on Iran, which may be of some use to you in your efforts to assist the asylum applicants.

                Sincerely,

                STEPHEN J. SOLARZ
                Member of Congress

SJS:dc/g

Enclosure

1. Title I Programs – 75% of the allocations to non-public schools are administered through Central Board of Education New York City.

>   Contact: Mr. Marvin Barondes
>   New York City Central Board of Education
>   110 Livingston Street
>   Brooklyn, New York 11201

2. Title IV-B – Funds for library resources and instructional materials can be obtained if the National Committee for Furtherance of Jewish Education is categorized as a non-public school. If this is the case, the Committee may request funds through its local educational agency.

3. The State Education Department's Bureau of Bilingual Education is available to provide technical assistance in English as a Second Language (ESL) through workshops for personal or individual consultation to the National Committee. ESL materials amy also be borrowed from the Bureau. Technical assistance from the Bureau of Bilingual Education may be secured by writing to Gloria Casar, Bureau of Bilingual Education, Two World Trade Center, Room 5040, New York, New York 10047.

4. New York City Community Districts 17 and 18, located in sections of Brooklyn where the Iranian Jewish students reside, have bilingual education programs funded through ESEA Title VII and Chapter 720 of the Laws of 1973. The programs are designed for students who are Haitian and Spanish speaking; however, personnel at these schools are familiar with ESL programs and the needs of non-English speakers. The prime contacts in these two school districts are:

>   Mr. Lawrence Kushner          Mr. Harvey Garner
>   District 17                   District 18
>   2 Linden Boulevard            755 E. 100th Street
>   Brooklyn, New York 11226      Brooklyn, New York 11236
>   212-464-4900                  212-257-7500

IRANIAN JEWS OF AMERICA, INC.
P. O. Box 57345
Washington, D.C. 20037

The following is a verbatim translation of an antisemitic leaflet
circulating in Iran.  A copy of the original in Farsi is attached.


WARNING

TO THE IRANIAN JEWS


You bloodsucking people who have sucked the blood of every Moslem, have
intruded in our Islamic country and through loan sharking, theft, and
fraud have transferred the assets of the Moslem people to the Zionist
State of Israel.

You have taken posession of houses, properties, and shops of us, the
homeless Moslems, and have daily inflated the real estate values.

Now your golden dreams are over.  Therefore, we are warning you to leave
this land at once or else you will face the extermination of all Jews,
young and old, whom we will massacre.  And we will ransack and take over
your posessions.

In each era the existence of a Hitler is necessary and justified to wipe
out the Jewish race from the face of the earth so that our Moslem
brothers in the Arab countries may live in comfort.

Time for escape is running out.


                                    National Front of Islamic Youth in Iran

**REVERE & WALLACE**

LAWYERS

SUITE 902

10920 WILSHIRE BOULEVARD

LOS ANGELES, CALIFORNIA 90024

FRANK REVERE
JAMES A. WALLACE (1937-1976)
F. JAMES FEFFER
CATHERINE M. ADAMS
ARTHUR J. CHAPMAN
DANN W. BOYD

AREA CODE 213
553-9200
824-2123

June 9, 1983  ב"ה

Rabbi Jacob J. Hecht
Executive Vice President
NATIONAL COMMITTEE FOR THE
 FURTHERANCE OF JEWISH EDUCATION
824 East Parkway
Brooklyn, NY 11213

  Re: <u>National Committee for Siani, et. al.</u>
     LASC Case No: WEC 065 182
     Our File No: 816-001

Dear Rabbi Hecht:

Please be advised that the Court has now continued this matter
for Trial to December 14, 1983.

When I appeared on the matter on June 8th, Judge Clinco asked as
to what progress was being made with regard to the written
apology.

While I believe that we will be able to keep this matter going
for some period of time, I would very much appreciate your
advising me as to the content of an apology which would be
acceptable to you. This of course should be without any limita-
tions whatsoever. Upon receipt of such an apology, I will
forward it to the defendants and let them stew over it.

Your cooperation in this regard will be appreciated.

      Very truly,

      REVERE & WALLACE

      FRANK REVERE

FR/jp

**REVERE & WALLACE**

LAWYERS

FRANK REVERE
JAMES A. WALLACE (1937-1976)
CATHERINE M. ADAMS
ARTHUR J. CHAPMAN
DANN W. BOYD

SUITE 902
10920 WILSHIRE BOULEVARD
LOS ANGELES, CALIFORNIA 90024

AREA CODE 213
553-9200
824-2123

September 2, 1983

ב״ה

Rabbi Jacob J. Hecht
Executive Vice President
NATIONAL COMMITTEE FOR THE
  FURTHERANCE OF JEWISH EDUCATION
824 East Parkway
Brooklyn, NY  11213

> Re:  National Committee v. Siani, et. al.
>      Our File No:  816-001

Dear Rabbi Hecht:

I would appreciate your early response to my letter of June 9th.

In order to maintain our posture with the Court, it is important that we at least submit to the defendants a form of apology acceptable to us. You will recall that it is our plan to have the named individual defendants execute a stipulation to judgment in the amount of $10,000 in addition to their execution of an apology acceptable to us, with the understanding that we will then proceed to hearing as against the corporate entity.

I look forward to hearing from you and wish to extend my best wishes for a good year.

Very truly,

REVERE & WALLACE

FRANK REVERE

FR/jp

**REVERE & WALLACE**
LAWYERS

FRANK REVERE
JAMES A. WALLACE (1937-1976)
CATHERINE M. ADAMS
JEFFREY B. GOLDSTEIN

WYNN WOODARD
ADMINISTRATOR

EIGHTH FLOOR
1875 CENTURY PARK EAST
LOS ANGELES, CALIFORNIA 90067

AREA CODE 213
853-9200

August 9, 1984

Rabbi Jacob J. Hecht
Executive Vice President
NATIONAL COMMITTEE FOR THE
   FURTHERANCE OF JEWISH EDUCATION
824 Eastern Parkway
Brooklyn, NY  11213

Re: National Committee v Siani, et. al.
    Our File No:  816-001

Dear Rabbi Hecht:

Further to our recent conversation, I wish to advise you that
two of the defendants, Malekan and Fakheri, have stipulated to
judgment in the amount of $5,000 and have executed a written
apology.  The third defendant, Siani, was not in Court on July
19, 1984, and accordingly, the matter had to be continued
further as to him.

In fact, the matter was continued to August 8th, however, Siani
did not show again.  Therefore, I have obtained another date,
i.e., September 17, 1984, for the trial of this matter.  At
that time, absent Siani's cooperation, I will attempt to obtain
the largest possible default judgment as against him.
Hopefully, in this way, some justice will be achieved.

Lastly, I wish to advise you that the judgment has not been
formally signed by the Judge as yet pending the outcome
regarding Siani.

I will continue to do my best to bring this matter to a
conclusion.

I hope all is going well with you.

                            Very truly,

                            REVERE & WALLACE

                            FRANK REVERE

FR/jp

September 19, 1984


Frank Revere, Esq.
Revere & Wallace, Esqs.
Suite 902
10920 Wilshire Blvd.
Los Angeles, CA 90024

Dear Frank:

Did we settle the case with our Iranian friends?

I would love to get this off the agenda before the High Holy days. I am sure
that you, too, would like to get rid of this pain in the neck.

Wishing you and yours the very best for the New Year and hoping to hear
only good news from you, I remain,

As ever,


Rabbi Jacob J. Hecht
Executive Vice-President

JJH/cs

פתחו לי שערי צדק
ואני ברוב חסדך אבוא ביתך...

*You are cordially invited to join us in celebrating*

*The Chanukat Habayit* ~ חנוכת הבירת

*Dedication Ceremonies*

*Of the New Synagogue*

*"The Persian Jewish Center of Brooklyn"*

16 Adar II, 5741
Sunday, March 20, 1981
11:00 A.M.

828 Eastern Parkway,
Brooklyn
(212) 735-0200

Collation following program

**Program**
Opening Greetings
Affixing of Mezuzah
Lighting of Ner Tomid
Dedication of Haichal
Address by Rabbi J.J. Hecht
Greetings from Students
Guest Speaker
Tefilat Minchah
Cantorial renditions by
Cantor Mansour Eliav

DIVISION / NATIONAL COMMITTEE FOR
FURTHERANCE OF JEWISH EDUCATION

*By Invitation Only*

RABBI MENACHEM M. SCHNEERSON
Lubavitch
770 Eastern Parkway
Brooklyn. N. Y. 11213
493-9250

מנחם מענדל שניאורסאהן
ליובאוויטש

770 איסטערן פּאַרקוויי
ברוקלין, נ. י.

By the Grace of G-d
Erev Purim, 5741
Brooklyn, N.Y.

To All Participants in the
Chanukat Habayit of the New Synagogue
"The Persian Jewish Center of Brooklyn"

Greeting and Blessing:

I was very pleased to be informed of the Chanukat Habayit of the New
Synagogue and Center , which is to take place on the day after Shushan
Purim, and may G-d grant that it should be with utmost Hatzlachah.

The importance of the event, as well as its timely relevance to Purim,
are self-evident. As everybody knows, the Miracle of Purim occurred
in Persia, as related in detail in Megilat Esther. And ever since, "these
days (of Purim) are remembered and observed"every year by all Jews
everywhere - in the spirit of the first Purim, which brought about a re-
newal and resurgence of Jewish commitment to the Torah and Mitzvot,
as if they had just been received from G-d at Sinai.

What makes the event even more relevant is the fact that the new Synagogue
and Center will serve the spiritual needs of the Persian Jewish children
in the area. For, as our Sages tell us, the Miracle of Purim was brought
about by the Jewish children in Persia in those days, who bravely disre-
garded the threats by the wicked Haman, and gathered around Morchai
Hayehudi to study Torah, absolutely determined "not to kneel nor bow down"
to any force that would alienate Jews from the way of the Torah.

By the Grace of G-d we live here in a country where Jews do not face a
Haman. But the forces of alienation are nevertheless very strong and very
active. We must therefore do all we can to ensure that all our Jewish
children will be able to resist the influences of the environment, and will
always remain devoted and dedicated to the Jewish way of the Torah and
Mitzvot.

The new synagogue and center is certainly a notable achievement in this
direction, and a source of great rejoicing, not only for the Persian Jewish
community, but for all our Jewish people. And through redoubled efforts
to provide Torah-true education for all Jewish children and to spread and
strengthen Yiddishkeit in general, we are assured of "Light, joy, gladness,
and honor" in the fullest sense of these terms, and of speeding the true and
complete Geulah through Mashiach Tzidkeinu very soon indeed.

With esteem and blessing M. Schneerson

ב״ה

You are respectfully requested to participate
in the Third Annual
Azkara gathering and memorial service
honoring the late
Habib Elghanian
of revered memory
Thursday evening, May 14th, 1981
ביום חמישי, עשרה באייר, ה׳תשמ״א

at eight o'clock in the evening
at The Persian Jewish Center of Brooklyn
"Habib Elghanian Synagogue"
828 Eastern Parkway
Brooklyn, New York


Program: Unveiling of Tablet
Arvit Service
Cocktails
Presentation of Awards

R.S.V.P. 735-0200

מזל - טוב

יעקב

בה

You are cordially invited to attend
the Bar Mitzvah of:

YAAKOV  ABISHOR

Shabbos,

**טז סיון - פ׳ בהעלתך**

May 31, 1980

At: Cong. Yeshivah Rabbi Meir Simcha
Hacohen of East Flatbush
(Rabbi Hecht's Shul)
289 E. 53rd. Street

Davening will start at 9:15
Kiddush will follow davening.

✿✿✿✿✿✿✿✿✿✿✿✿✿✿✿

בה

מدين وسيله از دوستان محترم صمیمانه دعوت
می‌شود که برای برگذاری جشن " بر میتصوای " دوست
عزيز يعقوب ابيشور در روز:

شبات

**טז סיון - פ - בהעדתך**

در کنگرهٔ یشیوای ربای مئیر سیمحا کهن
(کنیسای ربای حقت) به آدرس:

289 E. 53rd St.
Brooklyn N.y.

حضور به هم رسانید.
شروع نقیلا در ساعت 9:15
کیدوش پس از نقیلا.

Rabbinical Court
New York

בית דין צדק
ניו יורק

147-0276th Road Flushing NY 11367   347-415-5681

Rabbi Eliyahu Ben-Chaim, Chairman

הרבנים להזדווגות לרב הגאון הרב הגדול צ אילותנו
בקרב ידידי פרס ההלותי אשרת בקודש בקהלות פרס
לבל המהפק להגיעו את צליות חותנו לשלון בבון
אולש ההד והרוסף הרג הגדול ומצלו לבולשו את הצדר
לקרא לאקוף מבעותם צובר שלו שית לצלו במפרות ספ
לשותר המהבק הם לב לצ שלי להיות הצרר לו
והגיוו אולת להיות שם הבאלים לאומריקה היום הכלורית
לאה ת צ אולותתם לשולרו הבלורים היה אירתן ומצלו
הסגר פלש ילות ולראשו להם בעולד את בלוו הם קיבלו
האיתרה הברית ואהה השלאית הרצם שלהל ואת ב
וכן לסיש פצולתם הצול שלו חייהיב להוקיר לצבוו
חרפו ואאבו ו תפולכו אבו שלקון אלרזו יהו שליקו
לשמ שליבו הל מיש רב קהלת הילצלו לצלהב האתיון

ב"ה

**RABBI YEDIDIA EZRAHIAN**

Chief Rabbi of Former Residents of Iran

**New York**

הרב ידידיה אזרחיאן

הרב הראשי ליוצאי אירן

ניו יורק

מכתב הוקרה

הפיא לפני האי אברא הבא חסיד ביקר אורין הר אורין אשבה הרבם יצוף,
הרב האיק נשלום הכל שלום, ובפים עמפך שאנבן לאופיא לאות הזהה ית
שינעו הכל אאה שהתב של אותו נשואל לפרם שנעם לפן אהבכג איש גא,
הם אמוהר הכל סאם, ויהי היכר הרב הכל ברום קנוב שהוהכן נובאן של
נאנר ובקש אקמל לשלום אג תלצירים הגוום 15-25 אמעל אמונה,
ואה לפים ואה הסוג כפולפן לשער בישביהב ועושי קנוה של היהדום שלאשנו אוה
לושאינו קנוש. הרב שלם בבר ההרהבר של שעי בארת האמסתה ד
חינק ה והני של שעשה שלום אל האפולין. שאית שפתי עיום שנואה יום לאי,
כשונו לאהיהב בהחתות אהסבכה היאלאוס באירן, הרב שלום הכל בארא אובין
העולא הליהי יצרקה הכל של. שבאו אאנה בקבלא פן אהאריא חמפם שהאישו
אאורן כא אתן לצירים וכושו אוג כנפהוס בהרכנים אומא לישוהב ם הב
באא אתיהם ולהינותם האאנהא הישובה. ובכו וטרתן שאוף אאוב לו ישואה
כבי. שהבצירירים לאהן האאנהה ובהה חבב.

חוה שנל אלה הרב שלום הכל כנל אאאוני קהולוך אלצאו אורא הרואהבוהאשא הפורשא
הדל, כאא לפם וגו לרם הרוחלוב שנישאולש יתהיף של אוהב גוד אגן,
והרי בשאי וכשם קחך לנצא צורא שאני אקרב לב לוביבי הבי יצרה הכ של
שם לכל היקר הרב שלום שלובא ואאאקל אל שלום להואב אוהק יאום הכאום הרהו.
בנג של חתלום היום היופן כן לאהבש אני אהבולהנול. שנא קראש.

הכהוב רב לגשי אובר היך ובירה אגא

15 North Road Great Neck, New York 11024   Tel. – Fax : (516) 466-4037

B"H

BHEROOZ KHANIAN
HADAR HATORAH
824 Eastern Parkway
Brooklyn, N. Y. 11213

December 3, 1979

Dear Rabbi J. J. Hecht:

My dear father, I am one of the Iranian students that are
studying in your school. My name is Bherooz Khanian and in Iran
I was in Engineering School. I have been studying Architecture
in Iran about two and a helf years and I have 73 credits in
this major. I love this major and my wish is to continue this
mojor and to build a Shule for my people. But, unfortunately, my
situation is not good and my father is sick in Iran and he can't
send enough money for me to continue my education. I need to
get a scholarship and I hope you will help me.

You helped us come out of Iran and you helped us to learn
Jewish Education and English. Please make it complete and help
me so that I can continue my education in college. I hope to
be a useful person for this society and Jewish People.

Thank you.

April 24, 1980

Rabbi Jacob J. Hecht
824 Eastern Parkway
Brooklyn, New York 11213

Dear Rabbi Hecht,

I am one of the Iranian students who came to the U.S.A. through your efforts and not only your efforts made me to come to the U.S.A. and leave the crisis in Iran with Ayatollah Khomeini and the other Moslems, but also your efforts made it possible for me to think that I am Jewish and being Jewish is more important than anything else. By staying half a year in Crown Heights I had an opportunity to see what it means to be Jewish, and to observe Shabbos. To be a Jew and not a Moslem is very important and I believe you and your organization are the only ones who made it possible for me to have the pleasure of being a real Jew. Although I am not living in Crown Heights right now but I'll always remember your kindness and special attention that you had given to me. Now when I think, I see that only a Jew could be so nice as you were.

By sending this letter to you I would like to express my appreciation to the Lubavitcher REBBE and you (NCFJ) and your family as well. Nothing in this world could be able to thank you for what you have done. I would like you to accept my best wishes.

Now I am following my Torah education here in America, the education which its foundation was built by you. And for that I am really thankful. Now, here I don't have my parents with me, but instead I have Torah and I feel closer to G-d. I wish you more success in your way.

Truly yours,

Daniel Haqzadeh

# Acknowledgments
൭൏

*A*bout ten years ago I was approached by my daughter, Sarah Deitsch, Co-Director of the Schottenstein Chabad House at Ohio State University, who asked me to tell her the story of the Iranian exodus. In answer to her question I sat down and began to write my recollections, which ultimately became the basis for the present volume. At that time, the Executive Secretary in the NCFJE office was Lena Silverstein. My first acknowledgment has to be to thank her for the attention and dedication she put into transcribing the material, some in the form of audio recordings, that I had originally prepared for the book.

When I subsequently decided to expand the manuscript, I delved into our archives to explore the files, notes, formal letters, legal documents, and personal correspondence that we produced during the years 1978–1981. Perusing those materials brought back vivid memories and gave me a clear perspective on the extraordinary events that took place in the process of bringing the Iranian students to America and caring for them in Crown Heights. Special thanks are due to Shimon Sabol, who is in charge of the archives at the NCFJE.

More recently, the technical work of transcribing, editing, and restoring additional material for the book was faithfully undertaken by Ms. Esther Bobroff, who is currently a member of the secretarial staff at the NCFJE offices. Thanks also to Mrs. Yardena Lipskier who assisted Esther in these various responsibilities, and to Mrs. Nazy Kavian, who helped coordinate many tasks essential to the completion of the work.

I would be remiss if I were to fail to express my profound appreciation to the many generous souls who were so deeply involved "in the trenches" and behind the scenes: those who served the Iranian students as *madrichim*—counselors, mentors, and tutors—during those intense few years at the outset of the operation; our outstanding faculty in all our educational endeavors; those who hosted and fed the students in their homes and in our kitchens; the enthusiastic and dedicated supporters—whether as connectors, advisors, or donors—in Iranian Jewish communities everywhere, from Forest Hills to Tehran and back again. This includes those who have been mentioned in my text, along with many more whose essential and often courageous contributions have remained anonymous, and unsung.

Special thanks to Mr. Simcha Gottlieb, a long-time associate of the organization and friend of the Hecht family, who embraced the challenging task of editing my manuscripts and preparing the material for publication. He has added a great deal to the structure, tone, and rhythm of the text.

Finally, my unending gratitude to my wife, Rebbetzin Channah Hecht, who never ceases to amaze me in her unwavering efforts and commitment to strengthening Yiddishkeit with true joy and fulfillment on a daily basis. She has devoted many, many hours to reading through the galleys and offering her insightful opinions and suggestions. I must also mention that she has a unique understanding of all that transpired during those years. While I was occupied day and night, tethered to our center of operations in Crown Heights, often returning home long past midnight after days that began before dawn, she heroically and gracefully bore the weight of the responsibilities to our large family and our Queens community, all on behalf of the Persian students embarking on their new lives in the United States.

# INDEX
ᘓᘍ

Page numbers in *italics* indicate photographs in insert following page 90.

# About the Authors
ᏩᏀᎵ

RABBI JACOB J. ("J.J.") HECHT, of blessed memory, was a third generation American, educated in
Yeshivot Chaim Berlin, Torah Vodaath, and Tomchei
Tmimim Lubavitch. Upon receiving his ordination
he served as pulpit Rabbi in the largest Orthodox
Synagogue in East Flatbush, Brooklyn, and in the
early 1940's was appointed to head the National
Committee for Furtherance of Jewish Education by
Rabbi Joseph I. Schneerson. Rabbi Hecht worked
closely with the Lubavitcher Rebbe for half a century; he was the official translator for the Rebbe at
all radio broadcasts of *farbrengens*, children's rallies,
and parades. A dynamic orator and popular radio
personality, he hobnobbed with public officials,
governors and presidents in his role as an activist

in many community, national, and international issues. The father of twelve children (two adopted), he was a teacher and mentor to hundreds of Chabad emissaries around the world.

Rabbi J.J. Hecht was a man the Rebbe could always count on to undertake the most difficult (if not seemingly impossible) tasks, with passion, confidence, and unflagging self-sacrifice. Among his many achievements throughout fifty years of public service, Rabbi Hecht:

- Founded and directed children's residential summer camps;
- Operated innovative Released Time programs for public school children;
- Organized and directed college-level seminaries for men and women;
- Established Toys for Hospitalized Children;
- Created the Operation Survival drug prevention program in inner city Brooklyn; and
- Successfully spearheaded many charity campaigns on behalf of individuals and organizations in America and Israel.

Author **SHOLEM BER HECHT** was there each step of the way, overseeing every facet of the operation under the direction of his illustrious father, Rabbi Jacob J. Hecht o.b.m., and the visionary guidance of the Lubavitcher Rebbe. A noted educator and spiritual leader, he is CEO of the National Committee for Furtherance of Jewish Education, Rabbi of the Sephardic Jewish Congregation of Queens, Senior Chabad Emissary in Queens, and Senior Rabbi of the Sephardic Community of Queens since 1974. A lifelong teacher, he continues to teach his signature course "Torah U' Madda" in Bais Rivkah High School, Brooklyn. In this remarkable book he weaves together the thrilling tale of *Escape from Iran* with his penetrating insight into its history-making significance.

## About the contributor

Pioneering educational media producer **Simcha Gottlieb**, an accomplished editor, journalist, filmmaker, and author in his own right, has been a friend and colleague of the Hecht family and the NCFJE for decades in the field of Jewish education as well as public relations. His editorial and research expertise have helped make this book the exhilarating pageturner the story so richly deserves.